Windy Times

Windy Times

Günter Kunert

poems and prose
selected and translated
by Agnes Stein

 Red Dust • New York • 1983

The translations
Copyright © Agnes Stein

The translations in this volume were taken from the following volumes:

Tagträume in Berlin und andernorts
Copyright © Carl Hanser Verlag 1972

Camera obscura
Copyright © Carl Hanser Verlag 1978

Im weiteren Fortgang
Copyright © Carl Hanser Verlag 1974

Unterwegs nach Utopia
Copyright © Carl Hanser Verlag 1978

Abtötungsverfahren
Copyright © Carl Hanser Verlag 1980

Die Beerdigung findet in aller Stille statt
Copyright © Carl Hanser Verlag 1977

Warnung von Spiegeln
Copyright © Carl Hanser Verlag 1970

Warum schreiben
Copyright © Carl Hanser Verlag 1976

All rights reserved

Printed in the United States of America

Library of Congress Catalogue Card Number: 82-061246

ISBN 0-87376-042-5

The translator wishes to acknowledge the editorial contribution of Joanna Gunderson and the close reading of the translation given by Christa Merkes.

The publication of this book was made possible by grants from the New York State Council on the Arts and from the National Endowment for the Arts in Washington, a Federal Agency.

All Kunert's works carry a dedication to his wife Marianne. The following dedications are from the works used in this volume:

Dedication to M: a poem
Warnung von Spiegeln

Dedicated most appropriately
to Marianne
Im weiteren Fortgang

A Dedication to the most important
cat painter from Berlin-Buch and surroundings
Drei Berliner Geschichten

Marianne,
the partner and
therapeutic agent of
my woes and fears
Unterwegs nach Utopia

Dedicated to a certain Berlin woman, born in
Reinickendorf, brought up in Heiligensee, moved to
Treptow, living in Buch, and nowhere else at home
Camera obscura

To Marianne, fellow citizen
between two camps
Abtötungsverfahren

Contents

Introduction: Self-Portrait in Refracted Light
(Selbstporträt im Gegenlicht) from *Tagträume in Berlin und andernorts*.[1]   1

I. *Foreign Body*   5

   from *Camera obscura*
      Androids (Androiden)   7

   from *Im weiteren Fortgang*
      In the Garden Late (Im Garten, schon spät)   8
      Domestic Afternoon (Häuslicher Nachmittag)   10
      Garden Path II (Gartengang II)   12
      Deserted Gardens (Verlassene Gärten)   14
      Old Photo, Old Street (Altes Foto, alter Strasse)   16
      Lost (Verlaufen)   18

   from *Unterwegs nach Utopia*
      Photo Album II (Fotoalbum II)   20
      Last Garden Day (Letzter Gartentag)   22
      Autumn Poem (Herbstgedicht)   24
      Likeness of Day (Abbild vom Tage)   26
      Sermon (Predigt)   28
      Nature II (Natur II)   30
      Moment (Augenblick)   32
      Structures (Bauwerk)   34
      Marks of Mortality (Kennzeichen des Todes)   36

[1] All German works in the Carl Hanser Verlag, Munich.

Sunflower (Sonnenblume)	38
Memory V (Erinnern V)	40
Summer (Sommer)	42

from *Abtötungsverfahren*

Foreign Body (Fremdkörper)	44
Arrival Home (Heimkunft)	46
Once in Thüringen (In Thüringen einmal)	48
Evolution (Evolution)	50
The New Man (Der neue Mensch)	52
In the Zoo (Im Zoo)	54
Surprise (Überraschung)	56
Spare Time (Freizeit)	58
Night Ride (Nachtfahrt)	60
Quiet II (Stille II)	62
Evening Song (Abendlied)	64
Elegy to a Distant Death (Todesferne Elegie)	66
Diagnosis (Befund)	68
Meeting on the Way (Begegnung unterwegs)	70
Impression (Eindruck)	72
Memory VII (Erinnern VII)	74
Later Nature Poem (Späteres Naturgedicht)	76
Speaking of Civilizations (Zivilisatorisches Gespräch)	78
Distinguishing Characteristics (Kennzeichen)	80
From a Breughel Background (Aus Breughelschem Hintergrund)	82
Memory VI (Erinnern VI)	84
Hopeful Moment (Hoffnungsvoller Augenblick)	86
Evening Poem (Abendgedicht)	88

from *Tagträume in Berlin und andernorts*

Cry of the Bat (Die Schreie der Fledermäuse)	90

II. Windy Times

from *Tagträume in Berlin und andernorts*
An Everyday Story of a Berlin Street (Alltägliche
    Geschichte einer Berliner Strasse)   93
Central Railroad Station (Zentralbahnhof)   98

from *Die Beerdigung findet in aller Stille statt*
Ride on the S-Bahn (Fahrt mit der S-Bahn)   101

from *Warnung von Spiegeln*
Fearful View of Future Situations (Gefährliche
    Ansicht später Stätte)   106
Specifications for a Golden Age (Indiz güldenen
    Zeitalters)   108

from *Unterwegs nach Utopia*
Windy Times (Windige Zeiten)   110
Sculpture of a Subjugated German (Skulptur
    eines unterworfenen Germanen)   112
Fellow Citizen (Mitbürger)   114
The Blameworthy (Die Verursacher)   116
Answer to a Questionnaire (Antwort auf eine
    Anfrage)   120
On the Way to Utopia (Unterwegs nach Utopia)   122
On the Way to Utopia II (Unterwegs nach Utopia II)   124
Poem after Benjamin (Gedicht nach Benjamin)   126
Biblical History II (Biblische Geschichte II)   128
Venice II (Venedig II)   130
On the Archaeology of Our Interment (Zur
    Archäologie unseres Verschüttetseins)   132
News from the Provinces (Nachrichten aus der
    Provinz)   134

from *Abtötungsverfahren*
   Near Itzehoe (Bei Itzehoe)   136
   Memory VIII (Erinneren VIII)   138
   Sleep (Schlaf)   140
   The Departed Speak (Gespräche Abgeschiedener)   142
   Before the Flood (Vor der Sintflut)   144
   Vista II (Durchblick II)   146
   State Visit (Staatsbesuch)   148
   Office Prayer (Bürogebet)   150
   Research Project (Forschungsauftrag)   152
   No Summer No Closed Season (Kein Sommer keine Schönzeit)   154
   Registered Letter (Eingeschriebene Antwort)   156
   German Elegy (Deutsche Elegie)   158
   News from the Antipodes (Neues von dem Antipoden)   160
   Berlin (Berlin)   162
   Motionless Moment (Regloser Augenblick)   164
   Mortification Acts (Abtötungsverfahren)   166

from *Die Beerdigung findet in aller Stille statt*
   Andromeda Out of Season (Andromeda zur Unzeit)   168

III. *In the Poem's Net*

from *Camera obscura*
   Memory of Scheria (Erinnerung an Scheria)   177

from *Warnung von Spiegeln*
   Nausicaa I (Nausikaa I)   178
   Nausicaa II (Nausikaa II)   180
   Orpheus I (Orpheus I)   182
   Orpheus II (Orpheus II)   184

Orpheus III (Orpheus III) 186
Orpheus VI (Orpheus VI) 188
Poem to a Poem (Gedicht zum Gedicht) 190

from *Im weiteren Fortgang*
Appearance Unexpected (Erscheinung unerwartet) 192
Latterday Poem (Nachgedicht) 194
So It Should Be (So soll es sein) 196

from *Unterwegs nach Utopia*
In the Poem's Net (Im Netz des Gedichtes) 198
Poem (Gedicht) 200
Fiction (Fiktion) 202
1974 (1974) 204

from *Abtötungsverfahren*
Clue (Spur) 208
Poem's Destiny (Schicksal des Gedichts) 210
Theatrum Mundi (Theatrum Mundi) 212
The Poems (Die Gedichte) 214
Pursuing the Poem (Dem Gedicht auflauern) 216
At the Dorothea State Cemetery (Vom Dorotheenstädtischen Friedhof) 218
On Dürer's Hieronymus (Zu Dürers "Hieronymus im Gehäuse") 220
A Poetics (Eine Poetik) 222

Epilogue
Letter to a Reader (Brief an einem Deutschen Leser) 225

Self-Portrait in Refracted Light

To present the real self: a paradox: how can one slip into one's own face without first recognizing that this is a mask and thus no longer one's own. Reflection estranges it. A complex matter—particularly for somebody to whom biography has made sense only as social paradigm and event. Even the writer who seeks to make clear that the so-called personality is a by-product of social circumstance cannot escape its all-powerful imprint.

Should I succeed in effecting this release of myself from myself (the way it might happen in the classic horror stories of R. L. Stevenson or Gustav Meyrink) I would view this creature in amazement: the way I sit at a bleached wood work table, gadgets nearby, virgin paper at hand, the round skull bared, mouth mustached, this figure with the melancholy physiognomy of a sea lion would appear even stranger than before. When I look at him, this Kunert, I must confess upon full reflection that I know embarrassingly little about him, very little of the essence of his being, and in general that my knowledge is limited to the external circumstances of his life, so that I must ask myself whether, perhaps, these external circumstances constitute his essential being, or, whether, as I sincerely hope, that what is wholly and purely personal has been pushed aside by these circumstances of his existence which are in no way personal. Favoring the side of the accused, I shall give the latter explanation the benefit of the doubt.

Moreover, I ask myself, seeing him there behind the table, bowed over pages of lined paper as if he were nearsighted, which he in no way is, does he have an independent existence, or is this figure not a metamorphosis of the lined paper made visible, since all paths of his daily life, his life as a whole, lead to these pages whose numbers decrease after an encounter with Kunert: the transformation of a ream of yellow paper into a human being catalyzed by the very act of writing on it.

But the writing process does not only change paper into a Kunert, it also changes Kunert into something—something which, in order to understand, circumscribe and explain, makes it necessary to cover this paper again and again with words in a script as difficult as Mayan hieroglyphics, so that he prefers to release new decipherings. But this takes place only later, after that transformation in which the uncertain psyche of the writer is again happily united with the external world—its totality and congruence of time, space, being, thought and sensibility restored—a state that has been thought of as the exclusive prerogative of the gods. It is a condition in which the frightening, crushing, foredooming constraints of time seem to end; in which time almost stands still: at the edge of this horrible abyss where it is only writing that stops the plunge. While it goes on, writing is a rescue from death. The moment of truth arrives when the individual gives himself over to his individuality and fuses his innermost self with the immortal I of the universally human—an I, which if it is not to be condemned to facelessness and disappearance, needs this balding individual, crouched at the table, bowed over the paper, to be made manifest and visible.

There is nothing much else of significance to add about Kunert: at most, answers to questionnaires, vital statistics, measurements and sizes, hat, collar, shoes. Of what concern are these to others: the wife to whom he is married, the friends necessary for talk and drink, the cats for filling empty rooms, favorite foods and favorite books, spaghetti with parsley, garlic and parmesan, and Arno Schmidt explain nothing of this writer I am, only that (with its specificity unspecified): Günter Kunert as Günter Everyman.

I
Foreign Body

Androids

I happened on a meeting of Androids. Highly interested, their eyes of the best crystal, measured me. Their lips whether of platinum or foam rubber greeted me smilingly. Their words could not be understood because they spoke with one another on a different frequency. I only saw: the way they looked at one another. I only saw: them rolling up a mechanism. Four, unbelievably strong, separated from the group. As they strolled on slow, steel rods out of my field of vision a chill grew on my back and neck. And not until I was locked inside the mechanism (too quickly for my snail-paced thoughts), and rotating nickle blades ate in my dulled flesh, did I realize: their intentions were kindly; they only wished to make me like them with the insertion of an artificial heart, a brain with programmed controls and a soul of technicolor.

Im Garten, schon spät

Vögel, leise plappernd im Schlaf.
Schnurrbartzucken der Katze
in ihrer unzugänglichen Abwesenheit.
Das unsäglich sachte Sichwinden
eines zufällig aufgedeckten Wurmes,
der im schönen Dunkel des Bodens
seinen ewigen Schlummer gehalten,
ein Traum reicht für sämtliche
Generationen: Wecke ihn nicht:
Störe nicht eine Ruhe, die wir verloren:

Hier dämmert ein möglicher Kronprätendent.

(Schöpfungskrone natürlich!)

In the Garden, Late

Birds, softly chattering in their sleep.
The cat's whiskers twitching
in unapproachable absentia.
The unspeakably slow winding
of an accidentally uncovered worm
which in the happy dark of the earth
keeps his eternal slumber,
a dream suffices for several
generations. Do not wake it:
do not disturb the peace we have lost:

Here lies a possible pretender to the crown.

(Creation's crown, naturally!)

Häuslicher Nachmittag

Vielfach tote Fliegen
auf dem Fensterbrett aufgebahrt
In ihrer Mitte
eine überraschend (für sie überraschend)
verstorbene Wespe

In einigen Fächern des Schrankes unsortiert
Teile meines Daseins
unbeendetes Puzzle

Vielfach sind die Fragen
die das Leben stellt. Etwa: Bist du
ein Grünling und ich möchte
erwidern: Auf immerdar.

In vielfachen Fächern begraben
die Briefe der Freunde
die hektografierten Sendschreiben
und Einladungen
zu den Versammlungen toter Fliegen
wo eine verstorbene Wespe traulich
allen was vorgesummt hat

Ich bin erschossen worden
von glücklosen Schützen
fahrlässigen Hantierern
Bist du ein Grünling und
ehe ich das abstreiten konnte
war es geschehen

Ich wollte nur sagen
auch in diesem Hause wimmelt es
von Leichen
die die Aussicht nicht stören.

Domestic Afternoon

So many dead flies
laid out on the window sill
In their midst
a surprising (it's the surprised)
deceased wasp

In several drawers of my chest
part of my being
unfinished puzzle

Many are the questions
life poses: Like: Are you
a novice to which I would
answer: for evermore.

Buried in my drawers
letters of friends
photo-printed circulars
invitations
to a gathering of dead flies
where a deceased wasp
sadly hummed something.

I've been shot
by luckless marksmen
negligent handlers
Are you a novice and
before I could argue
it had happened

I only want to say
in this house too
corpses swarm
and do not disturb the view.

Gartengang II

Da Holz: alt und rissig und rindig.
Eine Sonnenblume eine Abgesandte
ihrer eigenen Kerne
aus der Erde auf die Erde
und retour.

Es wird Herbst was bedeutet:
alle Pflanzen verabschieden sich.
Windstille und anderes Schweigen:
daß für Geräusche die Ferne nicht gelte:
da ist es Herbst.

Arme: alt rindig und rissig
wem denn hingestreckt.
Eine Abgesandte von wo an wen
zeigt ein Gesicht voller Narben
verlorene Miene und augenlos
klägliche Sybille.

Eine Eisenbahn fährt
uns ins Ohr und verläßt uns:
kein Aufenthalt möglich.

Lauter Unfaßlichkeiten
von denen nichts bleibt
als ein Verwundern dessen

den der kapitale Beton
entbarg: »Der Städter
in der Natur«.

Garden Path II

There wood: old cracked and crusty.
A sunflower sent out
by its own seeds
from the earth to the earth
and return.

Fall is here which signifies:
all the plants are bidding farewell.
Stillness of wind and other silences:
Where there is no rustling in the distance:
there it is fall.

Poor thing: old crusty and cracked
reaching out to whom.
A messenger coming and going
shows a face full of scars
a lost expression and eyeless
a pitiful sybil.

A train rides
into our ear and leaves us:
no stop is possible.

Numerous amorphous events
of which nothing remains
other than the surprise

at what the concrete marker
reveals: "The townsman
in the country."

Verlassene Gärten

Sachter Verfall wandelt die Farben:
Holz grau, Ziegel grün,
und das abgestorbne Gestein, in dem
kein Erinnern mehr glitzert, erbleicht
zu Kalk. Aus der Luft kommt
der Rost:
Ariel bräunt und rauht das Eisen,
dessen Jugendlichkeit uns sonst
befremden würde.

Unser Haus hat der Umwelt sich angepaßt
und entfremdet: was älter als fünfzig Jahre ist,
gehört zur Antike:
nächtlich in seinem Schatten kauert
Polyphem, blind und stumm wie die Gegend.
Das rückkehrende Licht vom Mond
bringt und wirft
alle klassische Spekulation, alles
metaphysische Fühlen in den verlassnen Gärten ab
und verstreut es unter die Bäume.

Aber was da gesät wird, geht am Tage nicht auf:
Weisheit pflanzt sich nicht fort: sie ist
das fruchtlose Ende, zu dem
jeder nur einzeln gelangt
auf seinem einsamen Weg.

Holz wird grau. Ziegel wird grün.
Weggehen und Nichtwiederkommen.

Deserted Gardens

Gradual decay turns colors.
Wood gray, brick green,
and the long dead stone where
memory no longer glitters fades
to chalk. Air brings forth
rust:
Ariel browns and coarsens iron
whose freshness would otherwise
estrange us.

Our house is adjusted to the surroundings
and alienated: anything older than fifty years
belongs to antiquity:
In its shadow nightly Polyphemus
huddles, blind and dumb as the neighborhood.
The moon's recurrent light
brings and throws out
all classical speculation, all
metaphysical feelings from the deserted gardens
and spreads them under the trees.

But what is sown there does not grow in the daytime:
wisdom does not spread itself: it is
the fruitless end which
each one attains singly
alone on his lonesome road.

Wood grays, bricks green.
Depart and don't return.

Altes Foto alter Straße

Sich einschleichen
in diese vergilbende Gasse,
kopfsteingepflastert, bräunlich
und menschenleer bis auf mich
und winke heraus: Hinter der nächsten,
für euch nicht sichtbaren Ecke
fahre ich sogleich mit der Pferdebahn
heim ins ewige Negativ.

Old Photo Old Street

To slip into
this yellowed alleyway,
cobble-stoned, brownish
empty of people except for me
and wave: around the next
corner not visible to you
I shall be riding off
home into the eternal negative.

Verlaufen

Echolos Erdenlos
Weinen und Greinen
Wo ist mein Fuß geblieben
Wer hat von meinem Mütterchen
gegessen

Rascheln in Büschen:
der Wind oder der Tod
rasch tritt er uns an

eh wir zur Lichtung gelangen
an die wir glauben
an der wir zweifeln:

Wo man den Wald
vor lauter Bäumen nicht sieht
verdecken welke Wahrheiten
alle Wege.

Lost

Echoless earthless
Groaning and moaning
Where has my foot gone
Who has eaten of
My mother

Rustling in the bushes:
the Wind or Death
quickly approaches

before we reach the light
in which we believe
and which we mistrust:

Where you can't see
the woods for the trees
faded truths cover
every path.

Fotoalbum II

Ein rechteckig begrenzter Hades
den du manchmal abends betrittst
aus einem ungewissen Verlangen
nach Vergangenheit

Schatten sehen dich
reglos an
In unbequemer Pose mitten unter ihnen
immer einer mit deinem Gesicht
den du zu kennen glaubst
doch das ist ein Irrtum

Es handelt sich um eine Figur
in verschiedenen Phasen des Rückganges
die eines Tages
unablösbar vom Hintergrund wird
(das erfährst du nicht mehr)
und die Gleichberechtigung verliert
mit einem verschneiten Gipfel
einer Welle oder bloß
mit den gestreiften Tapeten
von nebenan.

Photo-Album II

Hades with rectangular borders
where you visit those evenings
when a vague desire fills you
for the past

Motionless shadows
look at you
Amongst them in an awkward pose
always someone with your face
whom you think you know
but that is an error

It's a matter of a figure
in various phases of regression
that one day
(no longer to be yours)
cannot be distinguished from the background
losing its claim for equal attention
to a snow-topped hill
or a wave or just
the striped wallpaper
at its side

Letzter Gartentag

Hast du bemerkt
wie entgegen dem Augenschein
die Fliegen wie die Fliegen sterben?
Sommer für Sommer mißlingt
der Ausbruch der Wespen
aus einer ausgetrunkenen Cola-Flasche.
Die Blätter ringsum sind rastlos
und fallen trotzdem
wie du siehst und meine Hand
auf der Lehne ist eine unbeholfene Wurzel
nur für eine Weile zum Festhalten
geeignet. Der Schatten des Hauses
nähert sich uns unaufhaltsam
wie ohne Absicht.
Hast du
den schwarzen Falter bemerkt
jetzt am Nachmittag und daß er
aussieht wie Asche? Und
daß alle Dinge sich anstrengen
damit wir etwas wahrnehmen
was so wenig zu bemerken ist
wie die Bewegung der Erde
im Universum
obwohl genauso
unwiderruflich.

Last Garden Day

Have you noticed
how despite appearances
flies die like flies?
Summer after summer wasps
fail to break out
of the empty cola bottle.
All around leaves are restless
nevertheless fall
as you see and my hand
on the railing is an awkward root
only temporarily suited
for holding on. The house shadow
gradually comes closer
as if without goal.
Have you
noticed the black fold
in the afternoon now and that
it looks like ashes? And
that all things are straining
for us to take note of something
which is as unremarkable
as the earth's movement
in the universe
although just as
irrevocable.

Herbstgedicht

Massen von Licht
Das Licht der Erfahrung
an einem frühen Morgen im Herbst
Keine Bewegung der Luft
Kein Geräusch
Nur Klarheit

Für die späteren dunklen Tage
zum Nachleuchten

Für den gewissen Winter

Für die Undurchsichtigkeit der Welt
nimm etwas Sonne zu dir
nach trauriger Schildbürgerart.

Autumn Poem

Masses of light
The light of experience
on an early autumn morning
No movement of air
not a stir
only clarity

for lighting
those dark days coming

in the certain winter

Take some sun to yourself
to break through the world's opaque wall
in the sad manner of foolish wise men

Abbild vom Tage

Lange leblose Tage
Keine Miene regt sich
im Gesicht allgemeiner Abwesenheit
Ein ergreifender Stillstand
ohne Horizont und Ausblick
weil alles ringsum verdeckt ist
von brüchigem Holz im Geviert
das schon fault
unter der hilflosen Hand
Alles verdeckt von Blättern und Blumen
von Tafeln und Inschriften
von langen Sätzen aus kürzlichen Worten
hinter denen
du dich selber vermutest
aber das ist von allen
der dauerhafteste Wahn

Du bleibst nämlich der
den sie an den Beinen wegzogen
eine lange blutige Spur
die ganze Straße lang
zu Ehren der Tafeln und Inschriften
und anderer Irrtümer
für immer.

Likeness of Day

Long lifeless days
Not an expression raised
on the face of universal absence
An affecting standstill
without horizon or prospect
because everything contained here is covered
with brittle wood in a square
rotting
under the helpless hand
All is covered with leaves and flowers
with plaques and inscriptions
with long sentences made of short words
behind which
you presume to find yourself
which of all things is
the most resistant delusion

Because you're the one
they've pulled away by his legs
a long bloody track
the length of the street
in honor of the tablets and inscriptions
and other errors
for evermore.

Predigt

Noch nicht Asche
bist du schon zerstreut
und für dich unauffindbar

Verschüttet die Kontinente
von apokalyptischen Gegenständen
aus dem Gebein treuer Bürger
die zu leben glauben: Heilige
unserer Tage

Unaufgeräumte Spätzeit
kurz vor dem Dunkelwerden erfüllt
von Blech aus Fabriken
Rädern und Gedränge
von Worten die jeden überfahren
geregelt
ist alles längst
wenig noch zu ordnen
ein paar Einzelne einzuschwören
auf den Tod mit dem
klangvollen Namen

Nacht heißt die letzte Zuflucht
Finsternis und freiwillige Abwesenheit
Starr auf dem Rücken liegen bleiben
Die Flügel gefaltet
im Gebet um Vergessensein

Sermon

Not yet ashes
you're already scattered
and for yourself untraceable

Buried a continent
of apocalyptic objects
from the bones of loyal citizens
who believe themselves alive: The saints
of our time

The untidied end of day
shortly before dark filled
with fabricated sheet metal
wheels and throngs
of words driving over everybody
all has
long been organized
little left to arrange
a few are left
still to be sworn
into Death's solemn company

Night is the last refuge
darkness and freely willed absence
To lie stiff on one's back
the wings folded
in prayer for forgetfulness

Natur II

Dieses ausgelaugte Holz
und dieses frische der Kiefer

Nur zu bald überziehen sich im Gras
Ziegelsteine grün
der Mauergemeinschaft entkommen

Was dem Regen ausgesetzt wird
dem Wind wie der Windstille
Winter und wieder Wärme
wandelt sein Wesen indem es
sein zweckdienliches Aussehen aufgibt

Du seltsamer Sessel
aus geflochtenem Rohr auf vier Beinen
lange Zeit unterwegs und schief geworden dabei
abwartend noch oder schon ganz zukunftslos

Ihr Bruchstücke ringsum
für niemanden außer euch selber
versammelt:

Wahr ist die Welt nur
in allem was ihr nichts nützt
und: Den Ausgestoßenen allein
gehört der Mut zum nötigen
Verrat.

Nature II

This rotted wood
and the freshness of the pine

The bricks in the grass escaped
from the brick-work community
covered only too quickly in green

Whatever is put out in the rain
for the wind as well as the calm
winter and return of warmth
changes its essence as it
gives up the appearance of usefulness

You special chair
of braided cane on four legs
grown crooked in the long journey on the way
still waiting or already without a future

You fragments all around
collected for no one besides
yourselves:

The world is true only
in those things useless to it
and: The exile alone
has the courage for the required
treachery.

Augenblick

Für Augenblicke
steht das Leiden still
an dem die Zeit gemessen wird
als sei ins Räderwerk
das uns behaust
ein Splitter von Barmherzigkeit geraten:
Das ist der Irrtum unsres Lebens
den wir mit jenem
bezahlen

Stillstand für einen Augenblick
bildet bloß
vor dem erneuten Ineinandergriff
der Zähne eine Leere
für die wir immer ausersehen
sind und bleiben

Für einen Augenblick
der Traum: Es sei
der letzte des alltäglichen
Gestorbenwerdens
der erste meiner Auferstehung
und deiner selbstverständlich
auch.

Moment

Suffering by which time
is measured stands still
for a moment
as if a splinter of mercy
entered the gear works
that house us:
we pay for this
life's error
with life

Momentary standstills
only create a vacuum
before the renewed
bite of teeth
which is and remains
our destiny

For a moment
the dream: It is
the last of the daily
dying
the first of my rising
and yours too
of course.

Bauwerk

Das Gestein deiner Tage
eine unsichtbare Pyramide
überdämmert vom Ende

Das Gestein deiner Erdentage
umschließt dich eng
und enger
ärmliches Monument
unter dem du verwundert
verschwindest

Aber auch dieses Bauwerk
zerfällt und in Bälde
insichzusammen und hinterläßt
geschichtlich gesehen
keine Spur

Ein verschenkter Anzug
ein zerbrochener Sessel
eine völlig verrostete Uhr
zeichnen unverantwortlich für dich

Das Gestein deiner Tage
eine Nachgeburt aus Schutt
für Nachgeborene.

Structures

Building blocks of your days
an invisible pyramid
clouded at the end

The building blocks of your earthly days
enclose you tightly
and ever more tightly
sparse monument
beneath which you astonished
disappear

But even this structure
falls apart and soon
disintegrates and
historically viewed leaves
not a trace

A suit given away
a broken armchair
a completely rusted clock
a design indifferent to you

the building blocks of your days
after-birth of rubble
for those coming later.

Kennzeichen des Todes

Als sei der Mund nur
zum Schweigen da
Augen die nichts erkennen
Ohren die kein Signal mehr vernehmen
Steh' auf und wandle
umsonst vorgesagt

Bewegungslosigkeit
und leichter Gestank:
Schaudere wenigstens davor
und vor dieser Zutraulichkeit:
So beunruhigend wehrlos
das Haar ordentlich
die Hände gefaltet
vorbildlich
Man kann mit einem Toten
alles machen wäre dies alles
nicht rein gar nichts

Vorführen aufschneiden verarbeiten
oder verkaufen: Irgendwohin

wo jemand
einen Leichnam mit der Erfahrung
des Nichtseins gebrauchen kann
derer wir nicht mehr
bedürfen.

Marks of Mortality

As if the mouth were
there only to keep quiet
Eyes that recognize nothing
Ears that no longer distinguish signals
Arise and go
proclaimed in vain

Immobility
and a mild stink:
At least a shudder before it
and this air of confidence:
So disquietingly disarming
the hair in place
the hands folded
a model
One can do anything
with the dead as long as it
is nothing

Bring forward cut up rework
or sell: Anywhere at all

where someone
can use a corpse
with experience of non-being
something we no longer
need.

Sonnenblume

Der Neigungswinkel zur Erde
entspricht ihrer Demut
Schwankend und um sich greifend
mit schlaffen grünen Händen
hält sie sich aufrecht
Ihr Kopf ist schwer
von Hoffnung
Sie blickt zu Boden
mit vielen Augen und ahnt
nichts von künftiger Blindheit
die ihr schwarmweise zugefügt wird
in der Zeit ihrer Reife.

Sunflower

The inclined angle towards earth
corresponds to its humility
weaving and reaching out
slack green hands
it holds itself upright
Its head is heavy
with hope
It looks to earth
with many eyes and suspects
nothing of future blindness
it has yet to suffer: the dispersion
at the time of its maturity.

Erinnern V

Vom sanften Schweiß der Nacht
beschlagne Scheiben: Abteil
Gerüttelt Unmaß darin der oder jener
oder du selber spät unterwegs
wie ausgestoßen oder eingeschlossen

Lärm von Metall
Ein neues Mittelalter bloß
auf Rädern und auf langen Schienensträngen
und dann: Ein Halt

Vergeßbar nie: die Lampe
die alle Schwärze um sich sammelt
Dazu Gestalten
wie nicht von dieser Welt weil du
sie auf der Welt
nie wiedersiehst

Du bist nur in der Heimat
deiner eigenen Müdigkeit und fährst
zu keinem andren Ende hin
als diesem.

Memory V

Panes clouded with
the soft sweat of night: compartment
rattling as if someone or other
or you yourself traveling late perhaps
might be shut out or locked in

Scream of metal
a new middle ages but
on wheels and on long tracks of rail
and then: A halt

Not forgetable: the lamp
which draws all blackness to itself
and adds shapes
out of this world because you
will never see them
again in this world

You happen to be in the native land
of your own fatigue and ride
to no other end than
this one.

Sommer

In der Mittagshitze wenn alles schläft:
Die Katze leblos auf der Seite
Die Fliege im Suppenteller
Blumen im Stehen
Einwohner hinter verhangenen Fenstern
satt und erfüllt von Ruhe vor den Stürmen
die meist im Glase enden
in Mittagshitze und in Schlaf
damit ein Kind durch Wiesen läuft
ohne Spur inmitten aller Halme
fern im Vergangenen:

Von allen atmosphärischen Erscheinungen
die eine die etwas anzeigt
wofür der Name Herbst noch nicht
das letzte Wort gewesen ist.

Summer

In the midday heat when all are sleeping:
the cat lifeless on its side
the fly in the plate of soup
flowers as they stand
dwellers behind draped windows
sated and filled with peace before the storms
which most of the time end in the glass
in the noonday heat and in sleep
so that a child may run through fields
leaving no trace between reeds
distant in the past:

Of all atmospheric phenomena
the one which points to something
for which the word autumn
has not yet been the last word.

Fremdkörper

Irgendwann gehst du
ins Bett und wachst
irgendwann im Sarg
wieder auf oder auch nicht.
Warum deine Strafe
die Sterblichkeit ist
wirst du nie erfahren.
Ganz fruchtlos
hast du dich vor Äpfeln gehütet
wie vor Mord obwohl
irgendwann schien
deine Hand einmal fleckig
in einem Traum
der keiner war
aber jetzt einer ist:
Angstgebilde
Wildwuchs
in der Magengrube
Jammertal.

Foreign Body

Sometimes you go
to bed and sometimes
you wake or not
in the casket.
Why mortality
is your punishment
you will never know.
Fruitlessly
you guarded against apples
as of murder
once your hand
appeared spotted
in a dream
that has become
one only now:
Fear formations
wild growth
in the stomach cavity
in the vale of tears.

Heimkunft

Was für ein Land ist das
das wie nirgendwo ist
besonders in den nächtlichen Grotten
vereinsamter Bahnhöfe.
Viel zu wenig Licht. Viel zu viel
Regen.
Habt ihr jemals beobachtet
wie sie den Abteilen entsteigen
enttäuscht über die Ankunft:
Wieder nichts als Kälte und Nässe
als Dunkel und Rauch.
Wieder nichts. Wieder ein Traum
mißlungen.
Schon stolpern sie
über den eigenen Schatten davon
von keiner Penelope erwartet
in den Hades ihrer endgültigen
Heimat.

Arrival Home

What kind of land is this
which is like nowhere
especially in the late night grottoes
of lonely train stations.
Much too little light. Much too much
rain.
Have you ever noticed
how they step from the train
disappointed at arrival:
Again nothing but cold and wet
and darkness and smoke.
Again nothing. Again a dream
failed.
Already they're stumbling off
over their own shadows
no Penelope waits for them
in the Hades of their final
home.

In Thüringen einmal

Trotz des Sommers
ein eiskalter Mond damals
und wie er so tief lag
im Abendschwarz. Die Erde
nur unerklärliches Gehügel
und lautlos. Auch wir ruhten
und berührten
Teile unserer Körper
so daß die Ewigkeit stillstand
und der Moment sich von ihr löste:
Ein Schnellfoto

Als ich das hatte hielt ich es
für die Welt aber es war
nur ein Jugendbildnis
von irgendwem.

Once in Thuringen

Despite the summer
an ice-cold moon that time
it lay so deep
in the evening black. The earth
an inexplicable mound
soundless. We too rested
and touched
parts of our bodies
so that eternity stood still
and the moment broke away from it:
a snapshot

When I had that I took it
for the world but it was
only a youthful image
that could be anybody's.

Evolution

Erde und Steine
Sand und Geröll
Ziegel und Quader
Zement und Beton
und immer wieder
wir

Zwischen Mauern marschieren
bedeutet: Es geht voran
Doch es leuchtet kein Licht
wo wir sind für uns mehr
und das Dunkel kommt
aus uns selber

Aus blinden Augen
fällt Finsternis
bevor die Hand
ins Leere greift.

Evolution

Earth and stone
sand and boulders
brick and clay
cement and concrete
and always we
in continuous repetition

Marching between walls
signifies: life progresses
But where we are
no light shines any longer
and the dark comes
from within us

Out of blind eyes
darkness falls
before the hand
reaches into the void.

Der neue Mensch

Sorgfältig umgestülpt
das Innerste nach außen
so daß ich ganz neu erscheine:
Der neue Mensch
sich selber fremd
wie es sich gehört

Mein Mund verzieht sich unsichtbar
während alle Geheimnisse
als verklumpte Arterien
und wirres Nervengeflecht offenliegen:

Nur darum
ist freundlich zu mir jedermann

drückt mir die Hand
daß ich nicht merke
wer ich bin

The New Man

Carefully worked over
what was my inside turned out
so that I appear wholly new:
The new man
a stranger to himself
as it should be

My mouth smirks invisibly
while all secrets lie exposed
like clogged arteries and
confounded nerve strands:

That is why
everyone smiles at me
and presses my hand
so that I won't notice
who I am

Im Zoo

Verwandte mit lateinischen Namen
Gesichter aus Fell und Gefieder
Hände aus Leder und Horn
Augen wie Glas
daß man hindurchsieht
bis auf den Grund der Evolution
wo die einfachen Gefühle wohnen
Angst und Verlangen
alte und dunkle Schatten:
Dein Blick
kehrt aus der Tiefe zurück
fremd geworden unterwegs
und sieht dich selber an
als gehörest du
nicht mehr dazu.

In the Zoo

Relatives with Latin names
faces of fur and feathers
hands of leather and horn
eyes like glass
through which one looks
to evolution's farthest reaches
where simple feelings dwell
fear and longing
old dark shadows:
Your gaze
returns from the deep
grown strange on the way
and looks at you
as if you no longer
belonged to it.

Überraschung

Von meinen Ohren
hörte ich seit langem
nichts
bis sie mir heute
im Spiegel auffielen
Ammonshörnern nur ähnlich
aber versteinert genauso
denn sie haben
mich nicht gewarnt
und nun wächst
dienstwilliges Gras mir
zum Munde herein.

Surprise

For some time
I've heard nothing
from my ears
until today when
I noticed them in the mirror
only faintly resembling Ammon's horns
but fossilized like them
because they
did not warn me
and now grass roots
grow obediently
into my mouth.

Freizeit

Sollen wir noch einmal
den Wald besuchen
die letzten Bäume aus Holz

Wollen wir insgeheim
einige Worte tauschen obgleich
ich genug von ihnen habe und auch
dir deine nichts sagen

Noch einen Brief
an die Öffentlichkeit
einen weiteren Salto
über den geladenen Draht
Mortale Monade
rückwärts

Wieder denselben Händedruck
für die Toten
wieder ein letztes Glas
ein allerletztes Stöhnen
noch einen Krieg noch einen Frieden
noch mal ein Nocheinmal

bevor wir in Abwesenheit versinken
bis nie mehr morgen

Spare Time

Shall we visit
the woods once more
the last trees of wood

Shall we secretly
exchange a few words although
I've had enough of them nor do yours
tell you anything

Yet another letter
to the blind public
another break-neck leap
across the charged wire
mortal monads
backwards

Again the same handshake
with the dead
again a last glass
a positively last sigh
yet another war another peace
once more a one more time

before we sink into absence
until no more tomorrows

Nachtfahrt

Mitten durch die Nacht mit dem Wagen
durch die Abwesenheit des Planeten
selber abwesenden Geistes
fleischliches Geschoß auf Rädern
das fünfte Mitglied der Apokalypse
durch bleiches Gewölbe das still
hinter dem Rücken zerfällt

Kosmisches Dunkel
wie vor der Schöpfung oder auch wie
danach: Verlorener Glaube
an Kathedralen und Tempel
an Bahnhöfe Brücken Paläste und nicht
einmal mehr
an die verworrene Höhle Lascaux
wo ich mich einst dem Gestein verband

Nur Nacht noch
und ein greller Splitter am Ende
meiner Mühsal
von hier nach da und wozu
nicht wissend

Am Ende alles wie geträumt:
Die ersten solitären Lampen
das Pflaster und seine Gegenwehr
die Grüfte links wie rechts
all ihre Fenster schwarz versiegelt
und auch die Läden
gefüllt mit Finsternis:
Verbot der Illusion
erwacht zu sein

Night Ride

In the middle of the night in the car
through the planet's absence
and one's own absent spirit
corporeal missile on wheels
the fifth member of the apocalypse
through pale structures
disintegrating at one's back

Cosmic darkness
as before creation or perhaps
afterwards: faith lost
in cathedral and temple
in railway stations bridges palaces not
even there any longer in
the confusing caves of Lascaux
where I was once in thrall to stone

Only night now
and at the end a bright splinter
of my labor
from here to there and why
unknown

At the end everything as in a dream:
The first solitary lamps
pavement and its defenses
vaults left and right
all windows black and shut
and the shops as well

filled with darkness:
not permitting the illusion
of being awake

Stille II

Wortlos Stille predigen
und Schweigen erbitten
Einfaches Schweigen der Steine
die durch ihre Zusammensetzung
alles erklären alles verraten

Vielsagende Oberflächlichkeit

Wenigstens leise wie Regen sein
durch das eintönige Alphabet der Tropfen
trotzdem mit wem sich verständigen
über irgendetwas
in umfassender Flüchtigkeit

Du würdest verstehen
worum es geht wäre dein Ohr
nicht verwelkt längst vom Lärm
nicht taub das Hirn
von der Lüge.

Quiet II

To preach quiet wordlessly
and prevail upon silence
Simple silence of stones
that in their composition
explain all reveal all

Expressive surfaces

To be at least as hushed as rain
with its monotone alphabet
nevertheless to come to an understanding
about something with someone
within an ephemeral environment.

You would understand
the matter if your ear
had not long been wasted by noise
and your brain not deafened
with lies.

Abendlied

Wenn eine Schnecke denkt
sie fliegt
dann kann sie mich verstehen

Hier sitze ich im Dunkel
der Spirale
ohne klaren Ausgang: Sie gilt
für so zerbrechlich daß niemand
es zu beschreiben wagt:
Ein falsches Wort zerstört sie
und ihr wißt
das beste von uns allen
ist das Sediment

Daher die Gehäuse
die vielen Toten und
die vielen Zeichen
aus denen die Gedanken kommen

echolos im übrigen.

Evening Song

The snail that believes
it can fly
may understand me

Here I sit in the dark
of the spiral
without a clear exit: It is assumed
to be so fragile that no one
dare describe it:
A wrong word would destroy it
and you know
the best of all of us
is our sedimentary deposit

Therefore the casings
the many dead
the many symbols
from which thoughts arise

echoless moreover.

Todesferne Elegie

In ihrer Weinhandlung
in der Via dei Chiavari
in der düsteren Höhle die beiden Alten
sind vollkommen unsterblich
Ein korpulenter Silen
unrasiert unter schmutziger Mütze
eine aufgetriebene Dryade
mit dicken unbeweglichen Säulenstümpfen
anstelle der Beine
Kühle und Stille nur ihre Gefährten
Osmotisches Sein
gezeichnet von heiliger Reglosigkeit

Hinter vergrautem Glas
ein wenig Wurst ein wenig Käse
Flaschen ohne Etikett erwartungsvoll leer
säuerlicher Geruch von den Fässern
und kein Gruß und kein Lächeln
Kühle und Stille und Schweigen

ein erstarrtes Arkadien
wo *er* nie gewesen scheint
hinter der nächsten Ecke
des Campo di Fiori.

Elegy to a Distant Death

In their wine cellar
in the Via dei Chiavari
the old couple in the dark cave
is fully immortal
A corpulent Silenus
unshaven beneath a dirty cap
a raised up dryad
with thick immobile stumps of stone
instead of legs
cool and quiet her only companions
osmotic being
marked by a holy stillness

Behind the grayed glass
a little cheese a little sausage
unlabelled bottles expectantly empty
sour smell from the barrels
no greeting no smile
Cool and quiet and silence

A frozen Arcady
where *he* never seems to have existed
around the next corner
of the Campo de Fiori.

Befund

Unterwegs in einer Nußschale
oder in einem Schlaf von wenigen Minuten
durch das vollkommene Grün
sterblicher Natur: eine Expedition
in die Vorzeit deiner Person

Wenn die Sonne
gerade noch das kalte Wehen
polarer Luftmassen durchdringt
ein geädertes Blatt sklerotisch vergilbt
und dein regloses Auge am Okular
das Muster entdeckt
nach dem du gelebt hast

Vor Jahren hätte dir solche Kenntnis genutzt
jetzt jedoch siehst du es
viel zu spät: Keine Korrektur
mehr möglich

Dir bleibt die Nußschale hinfort
der Schlaf gütigenfalls
du selber bleibst bei dir
und so starr vor dich hinblickend
wahrscheinlich noch jahrelang.

Diagnosis

Traveling in a nutshell
or a few minutes' nap
through the perfected green
of mortal nature: an expedition
into your personal pre-history

When the sun
pierces through the cold sweep
of polar air masses
yellowing a veined sclerotic leaf
and your eye fixed at the oculus
perceives the pattern
which has ruled your life

Years ago such knowledge would have helped
but what you see now
comes far too late: no more
corrections permissible

The nutshell remains
and the benign sleep
you yourself stay at home
staring rigidly before you
perhaps for years to come

Begegnung unterwegs

Unter allen Brauen
und sonstigen behaarten Stellen

im kalten Zentrum unseres Auges
das das Fleisch durchmustert
seine Trägheit und sein Ende

in dieser vollkommenen Hand
dem einzigen Absolutum der Anbetung würdig
fähig zu allem

sowie im Widerschein des Abteilfensters
ist Gott inkarniert
Du unerwartet ungeheuer selber

während der Schnellzugfahrt
durch eine unverweilte Landschaft
nordwärts

Meeting on the Way

Beneath the eyebrows
and other hairy places

in the cold center of our eye
passing judgment on flesh
its indolence and its end

in this perfected hand
the single absolute worthy of worship
capable of all

in the train window's reflection
you, unexpected monstrous self
God is made incarnate

while the express
rushes swiftly through the landscape
to the North.

Eindruck

Um die Augen der Welt
eine Binde
Vogelgezwitscher bleibt
vernehmlich Blumen duften
absichtslos
Wind weht
Zu Sand zerfallen die Gebirge
nur zum Verscharren
der unbenannten Reste
nach den Salven

Impression

A blind
around the eyes of the world
Bird twitter remains
and the fragrance of flowers
purposeless
Breezes blow
The hills collapse into sand
to cover the unnamed remains
after the salvos

Erinnern VII

Aus dem Vineta der Kindheit
wird selten Glockenton hörbar
Jedes Begräbnis verläuft schweigend
Und betroffen stehst du
vor der kleinen Leiche
die du besser
nicht wärst.

Memory VII

Bells are rarely heard
in the vignettes of childhood
Every burial passes in silence
and you stand embarrassed
before the small corpse
it would be better
not to have been

Späteres Naturgedicht

Gitterwerk Bäume
Gefangenschaft des Blickes
waldwärts
Borkige Monotonie
mit Dämmer durchsetzt
von Stille verraten

Ameisenheere
kommen aus ihren Heimen hervor
demonstrative Züge
»freiwillig und freudig«
lag mir im Sinn
aber unter und über dem Laub
die Erde scheint taub
gegen die Wünsche Begrabener
vor ihrem Begrabensein
und ich ging über ihre Unzahl weiter
so für mich hin.

Later Nature Poem

Lattice work trees
imprisoning the view
towards the woods
monotony of bark
interspersed with twilight
disclosed by stillness

Armies of ants
are leaving their home
demonstration march
"freely and joyfully"
comes to mind
but above and below the leaves
it appears the earth is deaf
to demands of the buried
before their burial
and I step over their huge number simply
going my way

Zivilisatorisches Gespräch

Eine Tablette und noch eine
Tablette: schon verwehen die Jahre
erträglicher. Der Schmerz
über der linken Braue: Eingeständnis
der Sterblichkeit. Unendlicher Fall
grüner Blätter: die Menschheit
auf dem Marsch und du
sprichst von einem Leuchten
fünfzehn Milliarden Lichtjahre fern
und welche Bedeutung wir dem zumessen
in Hinsicht darauf
daß es wieder keine Orangen gibt
keine Freundlichkeit keine Freiheit
und keine Bücher über den Anlaß
solchen Mangels

Mein Lieber
die größten Dichter kamen
aus dem Neandertal weil sie
nichts hinterließen als Rätsel
Wir stattdessen
haben die Schrift
uns zu beklagen.

Speaking of Civilizations

One tablet and yet another
tablet: the passage of years
growing tolerable. The pain
over the left eyebrow: acceptance
of mortality. Endless fall
of green leaves: humanity
on the march and you
speaking of light shining
fifteen billion light years distant
and its significance to us
as it relates to the fact of yet again no oranges
no friendliness no freedom
and no books on the instance
of such absences

My dear friend
the greatest poets came
from Neanderthal times because
they left nothing behind but puzzles
we on the other hand
have written language
with which to complain.

Kennzeichen

Nirgendheim: Da kommen wir her
da fahren wir hin
Zwischen Glücksstadt und Freudenfeld
verhöhnen die Namen den Fremden
und das ist das bessere Los
statt untergehen im südchinesischen Meer:
Keiner versteht deine Sprache
keiner die letzte Botschaft
an die Welt so daß die Welt weitertickt
oder bloß währt

Verkannt
als Geste des Bettelns
deine ausgestreckte Hand eh sie fault:
Nichts bist du und nichts
wirst du: Matter Fleck
verwischte Zahl
stumm unter dem Zierat kleiner Meldungen

Das Aussichtslose: Du in Person
leer der Blick die Gefäße geschwollen
ohne Kraft des Kopfes
von keiner Hypothese vorgesehen
einer Legende entstammend
in einer anderen sterbend
versehen mit vielen besonderen
Kennzeichen

Distinguishing Characteristics

Nowhere at home: That's where we come from
that's where we're going
between Lucksville and Funfield
sneering at names of strangers
which is a better lot
than drowning in the South China seas:
No one understands your language
no one your last message
to the world so that the world ticks on
or just endures

Mistaken
as a begging gesture
your hand stretched out before it rots:
You are nothing and will become
nothing: Dull spot
wiped out number
dumb beneath decorative small notices

Hopeless case: your person
the glance empty the vessels swollen
head without strength
unforeseen by any hypothesis
derived from one legend
dying in another and
provided with numerous
distinguishing characteristics

Aus Breughelschem Hintergrund

Dieses alte Haus
in den Bildern der Ferne
umwindet für immer:
so spricht der Himmel zu ihm
Bäume und Büsche
kamen vor langem und bilden
seine Gesellschaft
Der wilde Wein hält zusammen und gurtet
die Kammern des Schlafes
dunkles Gekröse von Stiegen
die Küche inmitten
erleuchtet von Glut und den Blicken
der Katzen

Nicht einmal Krähen stören
dein Fleisch auf
Hier liegt es und wartet
nicht länger und dein Blut
speist Balken und Ziegel
und der Regen näßt deine Haut
seit Jahrhunderten oder auch nur
solange du es betrachtest

From a Breughel Background

In paintings of distant landscapes
this old house
eternally wound in wind:
the sky speaks to it
trees and bushes
have been here forever and are
its companions
wild vines cling and girdle
the chambers of sleep
dark clutter of stairs
the kitchen in the middle
lit by glowing embers and the eyes
of cats

No crowing of birds arouses
your body
Here it lies and no longer
waits and your blood
feeds beams and bricks
and the rain has been wetting your skin
for centuries or perhaps for no longer
than the time of your viewing

Erinnern VI

Wohlbehagen wohnt
an geheimen Plätzen
auf einem ungedruckten Atlas:
Ob es ein Kramladen in London
verwirrtes Universum
simpler Gegenstände
ob die eichene Dachkammer ist
ausgestattet mit Aussicht
auf Dom und Fluß und Fiesole
oder ein Bett für siebzehn Dollar
an irgendeinem Rand
denkbarer Ozeane

Orte alles
um dich zu verbürgen wie Traum
wie ein gelungenes Erinnern
wie ein Besuch
im endlich entdeckten Gral
verheilter Vergangenheit.

Memory VI

Well being inhabits
those secret places
on an unprinted atlas:
whether a junk shop in London
confused universe
of simple objects
whether the oaken attic chamber
fitted with a view
of dome and river and Fiesole
or a bed for seventeen dollars
on any shore at all
of conceivable oceans

Places all
made to secrete you like a dream
like a successful memory
like a visit
to the finally discovered Grail
of the sacred time the past

Hoffnungsvoller Augenblick

Alle Fensterscheiben widerspiegeln
Blätter und Gezweig
eines Straßenbaumes derart
daß es scheint es sei
hinter Glas
nichts als Baum Wald Natur
und die Fassade keine Trennwand
ein durchbrochner Mythos
überflüssig
zwischen Grün und Grün

Hopeful Moment

Every window pane mirrors
leaves and branches
of a street tree so that
it seems there is
nothing behind the glass
except tree woods nature
and the facade not a dividing wall
but a fragmented myth
superfluous
between green and green

Abendgedicht

Ach dieses langsame Einsinken
in den Abend. Die Erde
wird bodenlos sobald
ihr das Licht vergeht.
Noch treten die Füße Gras oder Schotter
dann nichts mehr.
Aus der Emigration des Tages
kehren die Toten zurück um raschelnd
in alten Fotos ihren Platz einzunehmen.
Jetzt zögert die Zeit wieder und täuscht
andere Zeiten vor: Welches Jahrhundert
hatten wir heute?
Ich würde mich nicht wundern
wenn vor der Tür Chamisso stünde
oder sein Schatten oder ich
sein Schatten bin oder auch Chamisso selber
der berlinwärts vor einer Tür
steht.

Wir wollen unseren Umriß verlieren
und glücklich sein wie niemand und zwar
Abend für Abend.

Evening Poem

Oh this slow sinking
into evening. The earth
loses ground as soon
as light leaves it.
Feet still tread grass or gravel
and then nothing more.
Emigrants from the day
the dead return rustling among
old photos and take their places.
Now time again tarries and pretends
to other ages: What century
was it today?
I would not be surprised
if Chamisso[1] stood at the door
or his shadow or that I
am his shadow or even Chamisso himself
standing at my door looking
towards Berlin

What we want is to lose our shapes
to be happy like no one and that
evening after evening

---

[1] North German Romantic poet of the 18th century.

Cry of the Bat

As they fly swiftly through the twilight, here, there, everywhere, their screech is loud but only they themselves can hear it. The tops of trees and barns, dilapidated church spires throw back the echo which heard in flight reports on the kind of obstacles that lie before them and where the way is clear. With their voice removed they are left helpless to find their way; bumping against everything, flying into walls, they drop to the ground, dead. Without voice they are overcome by what otherwise they destroy, now prevailing in increasing numbers: vermin.

II
Windy Times

An Everyday Story of a Berlin Street

Construction completed in October nineteen hundred and two: there its life began, deliberate, almost colorless, beneath the glow of hissing gas lanterns, under the patronage of a sun still thinly veiled; only later will the smoke begin to accumulate.

But its real history has a jerky start, in January nineteen hundred and thirty-three, with Herr D. Platzker, who is no Herr, but a human being in no way to be characterized by his name or his profession which he lists as "technologician."

From here on everything is determined by the fact that D. Platzker does not wait for the end, that of a speech, which someone else gives, Folk-Occupier by profession, an anti-human rather, who, in contrast to Platzker, will always be characterized by his name. We know who is meant.

In this speech there is a loud and strong reference to D. Platzker, which, if indirect, is of a threatening sort. And even as these gigantic blood-thirsty words thunder from the mustache-decorated mouth, Platzker secretly takes his toothbrush, some small change for lack of larger, and finally that most important worldly possession a human being may have: his passport.

Hat pulled over his eyes, he steps on the street completed in October 1902. He sees it lying there, poor but filled with rich expectations, similar to a hundred others yet wholly itself, and he can't bring himself to hand it over to a future, dark as the interior of a coffin. With the above mentioned jerk he simply takes it up. Rolls it up as if it were a thin runner, folds the roll in the middle and hides it under his coat. After all he's a technologician. Unfortunately he loses a few inhabitants in the process, among them the old lady from the tobacco shop who disappears without a trace, and all the birds twittering over the roofs in the middle of their flight.

In his ride across the border the street remains under his seat. At the border control it fails to be noticed as the search continues for more valuable things. Platzker's coat is removed as well as his hat and the D period is revealed as David and the real reason for the emigration. Yet he is not stopped from seeking his salvation in flight from calamity. Besides, it is when alone that every Goliath is most powerful.

Behind the border the tempo of the journey slows; it stretches out and curves, and soon extends over almost all of Europe, finally to ring faintly somewhere in the distance. So distant that exact information of the exterior circumstances of Platzker's existence is impossible to find. He himself is not clear where he has gotten and what surrounds him. This comes about because he is quickly interned as a German spy, or an anti-German spy, or sometimes both, so that before he can establish contact with the surrounding ethnological particulars he has already lost it.

Moreover this estrangement from the world about him can also be blamed on the street which he takes out immediately on arrival at the camp, an icy day, in order to use it as an additional coat in which to wrap himself. He succeeds only too well. He discovers its protective power against wrongs of the most discomfiting sorts; this derives from its unusual beauty, the inexplicable, dangerous, attractive beauty of the ugly. David Platzker is completely taken up by it. Nothing touches him as he immerses himself in the frontal decorations of the houses, in the apparently indifferent miens of fake cupids, cement caryatids, the expressions of plaster mugs which, from day to day, become more distinct and ever more like the gray faces of the street's inhabitants. In gloomy weather, the features of both living and composed models close up as if reflecting on what it was that led them so far from their native city. But when the sun breaks out and a strong ray of light passes over them, they light up like hope itself. Then the curtains in the windows are pulled aside, full-bosomed shapes are seen shaking out the bedding, or, in the half-lit rooms in which wine-red carpets may be glimpsed, there are indications of naked bodies in motion.

Unchanged the notices on the advertising kiosks, year after year; unchanged the men with the eternal blue enamel lunch pail in hand on the way to or back from work. Unchanged the busts of girls who fixedly remain girls. Punctually at night the draped windows light. With a buzzing sound the lamps on the Burgersteig at their hour start to distribute their powerful light.

At such times Platzker throws himself on a straw mat and the street under a board from which he repeatedly takes it out again.

Now it must be understood that he does not know exactly how much time he has spent on the camp's rubbish heap when he is told of the end of that man who was the cause of his departure; moreover of the end of the war and with that of his internment. He is already sitting in the ship, or, as the case may be, on the train or the interurban, when it first dawns on him that he will soon be home.

He wanders around in the remains of his city, and goes on and on until he finds his neighborhood. It is in his mind to put the street down where he first took it up: for, in the end, it does not belong to him. Besides there is a lack of undisturbed streets in the city and the return of this one would prove helpful.

From certain remains near the Frankfurter Allee he orients himself and recognizes the exact spot where the street belongs. When nobody is looking, he takes it out carefully, unrolls it, and spreads it between the scorched bricks of the neighborhood. But it won't fit, no matter how he draws it back or presses it down. It no longer fits.

Platzker has no idea what to do with this street; he was, after all, only its temporary custodian. It doesn't seem right to keep it. And because he is human and as such embarrassed by the unbelievable, he believes that if he now returns it unmolested and saved, he could possibly make his contribution to what, in a foggy and blurred way, is called a "settlement." Perhaps some day, he, Platzker, may even be thanked for it. With heavy heart he lets the street lie where it lies and runs back to his hotel. At night he can't sleep. The void surrounds him, monotonous darkness. Loneliness. He misses the street.

The next morning, having reached a grave decision during the night, he walks very early to the Frankfurter Allee and again meets with the remains that mark the place. Chalk messages cry out from broken plaster: *Where is Erna? We are still alive! The Children...*

Fragmented rubble rises, iron beams stick out, unrecognizable rods from which colorless rags flutter. Platzker looks around for his street when he notices that he's been standing in it all along. The window frames are empty, no naked, no full-bosomed shapes are moving behind them. The formless sky alone remains motionless behind the open rectangles.

David Platzker softly moves away from the street which he once possessed. Or was it he who was possessed by it? This can no longer be determined exactly. Moving off, his foot strikes a blue enamelled pail which, as it rolls away, spills a liquid which looks very much like fresh blood.

Central Railroad Station

One sunny morning a Somebody comes upon an official notice in his rooms; it lies on the breakfast table next to his cup. How it got to be there, nobody knows. Hardly opened, it strikes this Somebody with its demands.

You must, the official print on the limp gray paper commands, appear on the 5th of November of the current year at 8 A.M. in the Gentlemen's Toilets of the Central Railroad Station for the purpose of your destruction. Stall No. 18 has been reserved for you. In neglecting these orders you may be liable to a fine or punishment in accordance with the decrees of the legally established authorities. Light clothing is advised to facilitate a smooth transaction.

A little later the perplexed object of these measures appears disconsolately at the home of friends. Refusing all offers of food and drink he urgently presses them for advice,

but all he gets are serious and significant shakes of the head. Specific suggestions or offers of help are not in the picture.

Secretly, all breathe easier when the door closes behind this fellow with the sharply limited life, and one even wonders whether it was wise to have opened it at all. Does it pay, who knows what burdens they may be shouldering for a man from whom one can expect so little in the future.

And now he goes to a lawyer's office where it is proposed that he make an application to reverse the ruling. He is advised in any case to keep the appointment (Nov. 5) so as to avoid reprisals. After all the Gentlemen's Toilets and the Central Railroad Station have a respectable and reasonable ring. Nothing is eaten as hot as it is cooked. Destruction? That no doubt is a typographical error—instruction, not destruction. The lawyer finds it quite conceivable that the authorities might be concerned to give his fresh new client the proper instructions. Patience and trust! One must have trust! Trust is most important.

At home this poor fellow with his order to appear in the Gentlemen's Toilets rolls restlessly in his damp sheets. Filled with burning envy he listens to the heavy buzzing of a fly. It lives! It has no cares! What does it know of a Central Railroad Station? What does he himself know . . . In the middle of the night he rings his neighbor's bell. Through the peephole an impatient expressionless eye stares back at him until the bell ringer capitulates and takes his finger off the bell-push.

Punctually at 8 A.M. our man enters the Central Railroad Station, freezing in a short sleeved sports shirt and cotton pants, the lightest clothing of this sort in his wardrobe. Here and there an idle porter stands yawning. The floor is being swept while at the same time a sprinkling of some sort of fluid moistens it. His foot stops as he enters the shining emptiness of the Gentlemen's Toilets. He finds the door to No. 18 directly. He pushes the token into the lock of the door, it swings open, he enters. A wild thought strikes him, he is certain that nothing will happen. Nothing! They only wish to instruct him, nothing else! Soon it will all be over and he can return home. Trust! Trust! An euphoric feeling rises in his throat; smiling he locks the door and sits down.

Fifteen minutes later, two toilet attendants enter and with a passkey open No. 18 to pull out the lightly clothed corpse which they carry into the red brick depths of the Central Railroad Station, where, as everyone knows, no train has ever arrived or departed, although the smoke, presumably of a locomotive, clings to the roof.

Ride on the S-Bahn

1

On the outside, a wine-red surface smudged with black extending up to the window panes; from there a dirty ochre rising to the tarred roof. Compressed air opens and shuts the doors we enter with resignation, as if into a long expected doom. Inside, I roll along from station to station, unsuspecting and no more attentive than earlier. And am not aware: a window has opened like a wound. And waits. For me.

2

Although I have passed the brick guard-wall often enough, I never noticed the window. Perhaps it was only later that it appeared in the dark bricks; perhaps I was always sitting in the wrong spot. Or, was I one day taken by surprise as half-asleep, swinging along with the wheels, the out-dated cars on the worn tracks rattled me awake. Perhaps.

3

Only their names distinguish the stations whose sameness so colors the people that ultimately they cannot distinguish themselves from each other. And knowing this they hide their eyes behind newspapers during the ride, or let them sink to the floor that steadily moves onwards. One knows how one looks, how one has come to look, and saves oneself the trouble of glancing into the living mirrors opposite, there only for the duration of the ride.

4

On the bottoms of diverted streams from which the roofs of the city are scarcely visible we lumber on. Or, rising to the height of the second floor we cause all the windows on the street to rattle. High through the main streets or crossing them. Unexpected views.
The canal: red from the light of the sinking sun to the uninitiated; but for us who know and know, colored with blood. This is the water inextricably mixed with Rosa Luxembourg's blood as it flowed from her corpse. And on some days, silently traveling in his oilskin through the city, he remembers. But we not so much. We, so to speak, not at all. Resigned, our eyes on the tips of our boots. We count the rain drops on the window. We ride on and on. Unsuspecting that a light has gone on behind an unexpected window. And that everything else has become a problem of time and perspective.

5

Moving alongside houses. The noise of the ride thrown back at the riders. Precipitously the brick walls close in upon the curving tracks so that the traveller fears he will be carried right through apartments, chambers, living rooms, bathrooms, toilets, and finally discharged into a back room from which no train will ever come to fetch him. Brick walls. Walls. With their worn-away inscriptions they move into my face which is resting against the spotted watered pane. As the peeling letters reveal, many of these legends are from the days when advertisers were humane enough to address the local community. Isolated letters of the alphabet helplessly approach me and disappear, undecipherable in the rhythmic motion that carries and rocks me, and without understanding them, I understand: superannuated, vanished, wordy inscriptions incapable of leading an individual meaningful existence. Veterans of a beaten, buried, forgotten army.

6

One looks down, when one looks down, into the courtyards of factories which produce nothing but uniform days, into unknown abysses of the city into which our brothers have been thrust, these threatening rods of rusted metal; our sisters, the car wrecks; this is where our fathers rest, the broken rocks; our mothers, fragmented granite figures. From up above, and from view to view, they give the impression of old acquaintanceship; as if we had played between them and with them in the courtyards of our childhoods, since when, both they and we, we somewhat less, have deteriorated.

7

So between two stations. In the evening.

8

But one evening between two stations I, fully attentive, see into a lit window. Afterwards it seems as if this had been cut into the deep black brick of the wall; it glows, a singular break in the solid surface while I, this evening, between two stations, pass by.
The glance inside brief.
I immediately run to the back of the almost empty car in hope of catching another glimpse, even if only for a moment, of what I had seen. The train's speed is too fast.

While I run and run my eyes catch a corner of a darkly stained gleaming sideboard on which a white braided porcelain basket filled with red-tinged apples rests.
In the room itself, shooting so quickly past me, there hangs a friendly light in a silken shade, orange on the inside, green on the out, and there at the table I sit: smiling happily, an apple in the hand, a merry word in my mouth, I see it exactly, half-turned to someone next to me, a friend, who in fact is dead and long forgotten. There are several figures in that room; I try to identify them from the swiftly fading impression on my retina as the train slows down and comes to a rest at one of those stations whose names are hardly worth mentioning.

9

I rush over the solid concrete surface with its detritus of cigarette butts and paper shreds, left-overs from the days of the station's construction, to be preserved for archaelogists not yet born. Quickly across the platform and into the train which on the opposite side of the tracks is to make the return trip. My cheek pressed to the window pane, trembling, I watch the black brick wall with its rectangle of light approach. Come closer. Close. And there I am and notice first of all that I have finished eating the apple. And gone.
Among those present the faces were all familiar, not a stranger there. Many were long dead, burned or killed, or had travelled away or grown into old men. But here they were. There was a door in the room behind my trusting back, also lit, in which people were also moving, perhaps a little less clearly but as well-known to me as the others. A mood of peaceful, relaxed cheer pervaded both rooms and together with the lamplight an uncommon air of peace, such as I had

never known, emanated from this window. The entire rattling train of cars was already past the brick wall but the picture remained clearly before me, fading gently like the progressively yellowing photos in a family album taken at a time when it was still fun to store up memories.

10

I searched whole days and nights for this house whose narrow side was exposed to the passing trains. Often I stood in the rubble of courtyards and watched: would the train run by and past me? It could be I was not capable of finding the house; it could be it was so situated that with the best of wills it could not be found. In any case I never reached it. To stop the train in its course would be too unlikely an event and too dangerous. Between the tracks and the walls of the house there is a drop of several meters, a leap I cannot make.

There is nothing left for me but to ride the S-Bahn as often as possible. Once a week I make the ride, back and forth and again and each time in the swift passage I take what the room offers: the place where we are together, cheerful and real, living and dead and where we entertain each other with a lot of nothingness.

11

I know the train will carry me away from the window again and again. But could I once enter the room and join that self who will never finish eating all the apples in the porcelain basket, all that, which trainloads of words can never cover, would not have happened.

To enter once at the right moment would save me. And the whole city as well.

Gefährliche Ansicht später Stätte

Zur Nacht zur Ecke am Hackeschen Markt
im Frühjahr, im Herbst geh durch Berlin und hin
und erscheine nach der Jahrhundertmitte,
also geh jetzt,
da eine einzige Lampe hängt am Eingang zweier Straßen:
diese linkslang, jene rechtshin, beide
auseinander sich spreizend
steifes hohles Gebein gefallener Tyche, geschändete Greisin,
kahl und nackt und unverdeckt, bar aller Lichtflecke,
bis auf den Leuchtpunkt, da wo
das erstorbene Geschlecht wäre und nichts ist
als der Schwärze luftige Lava, ausgespien
beim Ausbruch, der eine Stadt verschüttet hat,
in der wir umgehen,
Kopien von Originalen, die weg sind,
ohne Zweifel an eigener Echtheit, solange wir
des Häuserwinkels aus pompejanischer Finsternis
nicht ansichtig wurden.

Fearful View of Future Habitations

At night at the corner of the Flea Market
in the spring, in the fall, go there through Berlin,
and get there after the middle of the century
so go now,
where a single lamp hangs at the entrance of two streets
this one to the left, the other to the right, the two
spreading apart
stiff hollow legs of a fallen Tyche, maligned old lady,
bare, naked and uncovered, devoid of light
up to the spot, there where
the died out sex would have been and nothing is
but the blackness of vaporous lava, belched forth
at the eruption that buried a city
in which we walk about,
copies of originals, now gone,
never doubting our own reality as long as
the angles of houses out of the Pompeiian darkness
do not come into view.

Indiz güldenen Zeitalters

Vorausgesetzt es geschieht
das längst Vorausgesagte und
aus dem verscharrten Gebein der Menschheit
bricht Licht,
Helligkeit aus Fels und Beton,
und ein unbegreifliches Leuchten sickerte
unter verschlossenen Türen, verriegelten
Pforten hindurch:
Auftakt der Epoche, die nicht mehr
vorangegangen gleich
ihre Finsternis mit Scheiterhaufen erleuchtet,
mit Flammenwerfern Leuchtkugeln Kienspan:

die Augen schlössen sich
vor solcher Blendung.

Vor solchem Glanz erwüchsen
der Erfahrung Früchte: Furcht und Zweifel
in den normverdüsterten Gemütern.

Aus güldenem Schein die Sintflut
die Schwemme gleißenden Gefunkels ertränkte
jede Hoffnung
aufs GOLDENE ÄON endgültig, fehlte diesem
als letzter einziger Beweis:
der Schatten.

Specifications for a Golden Age

Presume what was long predicted
has taken place and
light breaks
from the buried bones of humanity,
shining from concrete and stone
A mysterious light seeps
from behind closed doors, through
locked and barred gates:
Prelude of an epoch which
is unlike the past where
darkness was lit with the fire of burning corpses
with flame throwers fire-balls pine torches

Eyes draw shut
at such blinding

Such a glow brings forth
the fruits of experience: fear and doubt
to those already depressed temperaments.

In this golden glowing flood
the flow of glistening sparks eventually
drowns every hope
of a Golden Eon, for lack
of its final and only proof:
a shadow.

Windige Zeiten

Mit unbeholfenen Bewegungen
reagieren die Bäume
auf den Wind
Ohne Wurzeln würden sie
davonlaufen
vertrieben und fruchtlos
in regellosen Herden dahin
wo nichts und niemand
sie beugen will

Welche kahlen Weiten
auf einmal.

Windy Times

Trees react
to the wind
with awkward motions
without roots they would
run away
driven off and fruitless
in disorderly herds
where nothing and no one
can move them

What barren fields
suddenly.

Skulptur eines unterworfenen Germanen

Im schattenlosen Licht
der beigefügten Bildtafel
von keiner Witterung mehr
berührt
knie ich steinern auf Stein
das Gesicht geneigt
eine Hand erhoben
abwehrend
jeden Versuch
mich in die Geschichte
zurückzuverweisen
als eines ihrer Denkmäler

Denn ich lebe

immer noch in jedem
der mich für vergangen hält.

Sculpture of a Subjugated German

In the shadowless light
coming from the prepared base
no longer touched by disturbances
of weather
I kneel stone-faced on stone
head bowed
a hand raised
rejecting
every effort
to push me back
into history
as one of its memorials

Because I am alive

still in each person
who believes me gone.

Mitbürger

Jedermann kennt hier
jenen Mann und sein Bekunden
ihm seien Hände und Füße
wie festgenagelt
der darum nicht weggehen kann
niemand umarmen oder erheben
nicht lieben nicht kämpfen
nichts festhalten
und der trotzdem noch lebt
nebenan oder gegenüber
oder hinter deinem Fenster:

Allein von solch erhöhtem Platz
gewahrt man das Verströmen
der Hoffnung und der Tage: Oh
nehmt mich mit
nehmt mich doch mit
irgendwohin

Mag mancher selbst voll Mitleid sein
keiner kehrt wieder
weltflüchtig
und jener Mann bleibt da und hier
und stiftet auch weiter
Unglauben an.

Fellow Citizen

Everyone here knows
that man and his affairs
his hands and feet are
as if nailed fast
so that he cannot go away
neither embrace nor raise anyone
neither love nor fight
hold nothing close
nevertheless he still lives
next door or across the way
or behind your window:

Only from such an elevated place
does one notice both hope and days
streaming away: Oh
take me along
take me along
anywhere at all

Many may be filled with compassion
no one returns
fleeing the world
and that man remains here
and continues to foster
doubt.

Die Verursacher

Es kommen Leute mit großen Wunden
unaufhörlich blutend und tragen
sie in ihre Büros
in ihre Betten und in andere
mit unverständlicher Würde
schweigend oder bloß
örtlich betäubt

Es kommen Sterbende
und fallen in die Parkettsitze
Frisiersessel Bankreihen
auf die ständig verschmutzten Plätze
der S-Bahn
und verschwinden in der Abstraktion

Es kommen
unsere Brüder und Schwestern
Menschen und Unmenschen
sie schleppen ihre Seelen hinter sich her
verheerend wie Abgas
und verlieren alle Kontrolle
über sich an andere
Brüder und Schwestern Menschen und
Unmenschen

Es kommen die drei
apokalyptischen Begleiter
Hoffnung Zweifel und Gewohnheit

Es kommen täglich klägliche
Millionen

The Blameworthy

They will come: people
with large wounds
bleeding continually which they will carry
to their offices
to their beds and those of others
with incomprehensible dignity
silent or just
stunned in place

They will come: the dying
falling into their cushioned seats
hair-dresser chairs and bank benches
into the ever dirty seats
of the S-train
and disappear in the abstraction

They will come
our brothers and sisters
human and inhuman
dragging their souls behind them
devastating as gas effusions
giving all control
over themselves to other
brothers and sisters, men and
non-men

They will come: the three apocalyptical accompanists
Hope Doubt and Habit

They will come daily lamentable
millions

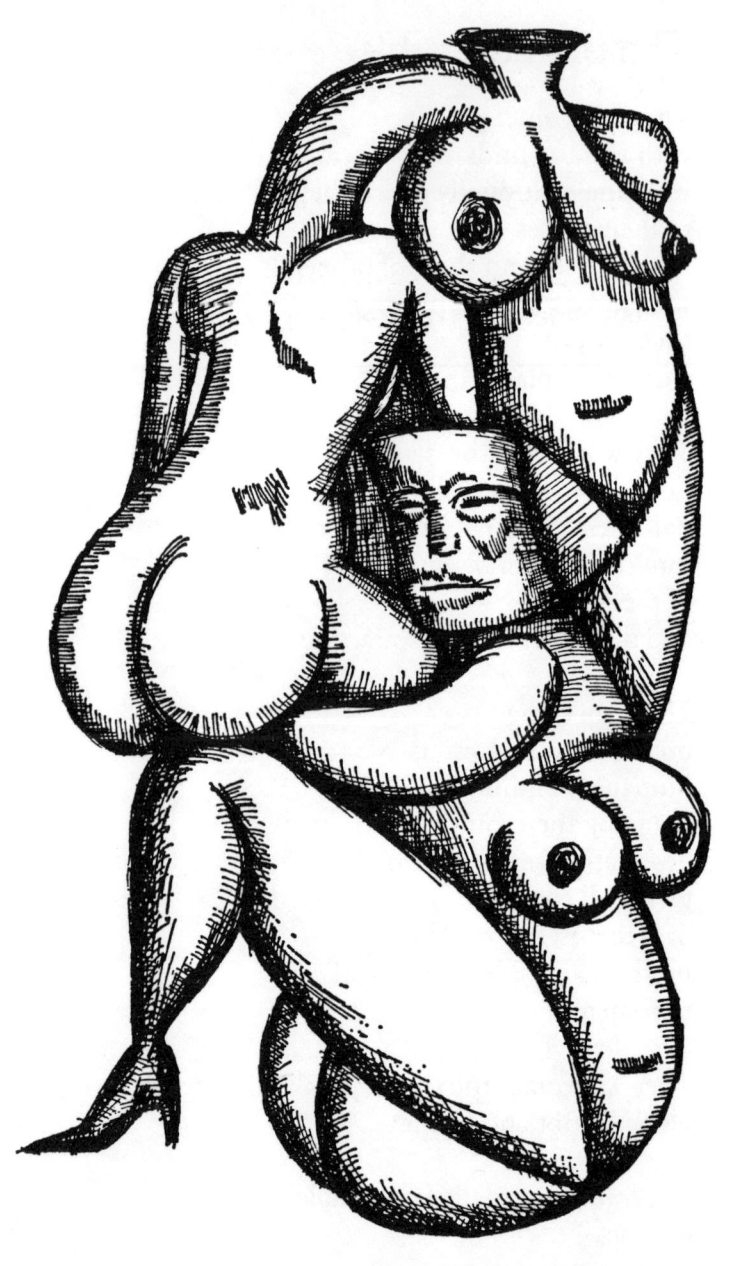

They will come more and ever more
they will step up and over
each other
to become a mountain
that one day will simply sink

in order to shape the familiar terrifying word
not audible not readable and
and and

Antwort auf eine Anfrage

Die allgemeine Hoffnung ist
daß es irgendwie weitergehen wird.
Wem die Haare ausfallen
braucht sich nicht mehr zu kämmen.
Die Anzahl der Verhungernden
ist in der Hauptsache eine Sache
der Statistiker
von denen manche eine Stunde
nach einer Befriedigung anstehen falls
sie dort wohnen wo
die Hoffnung zuhause ist irgendwie
ginge es weiter. Aber
die Rötung des Rundhorizontes
über den kärglichen Wäldern der Vororte
meldet der Spezies Morgenrot nicht.

Meine persönliche Hoffnung ist
nutzlos weil nur
darauf gerichtet daß mir
in meiner sänftigenden Hängematte
unter dem lichtschirmenden Blätterdach
daß meinen Frauen und Hunden und
meiner offenkundigen Nacktheit
nicht das Schicksal widerfahre
meiner fernen und stimmschwachen Brüder
meiner kurzlebigen Gattungsgenossen
im Dschungel Brasiliens zum Beispiel
begleitet von gleichartigen Tränen
aus den starren Krokodilsaugen
der Menschheit: das Verschwinden
in einem ihrer akuten Rachen.

Answer to Questionnaire

The universal hope is
that somehow everything will go on.
Those who lose their hair
no longer need to comb it.
The number of starving
is in the main a problem
for statisticians
some of whom stand by
for an hour after gratification
in case this is the place
where the hope makes its home: somehow
it will go on. But the red glow
on the curve of the horizon
over the sparse woods of the suburbs
is not announcing a pink dawn for the species.

My personal hope is
of no use for
its only aim is that I
in my pacifying hammock under
the leafed roof shielding the light
that my wives and dog and
my public nakedness
will not suffer the same fate as that
of my distant and weaker-voiced brothers
my short-lived colleagues in creation
in the jungles of Brazil, for example,
accompanied by the simulated tears
from the rigid crocodile eyes
of humanity: disappearance
in one of its yawning abysses.

Unterwegs nach Utopia I

Vögel: fliegende Tiere
ikarische Züge
mit zerfetztem Gefieder
gebrochenen Schwingen
überhaupt augenlos
ein blutiges und panisches
Geflatter
nach Maßgabe der Ornithologen
unterwegs nach Utopia
wo keiner lebend hingelangt
wo nur Sehnsucht
überwintert

Das Gedicht bloß gewahrt
was hinter den Horizonten verschwindet
etwas wie wahres Lieben und Sterben
die zwei Flügel des Lebens
bewegt von letzter Angst
in einer vollkommenen
Endgültigkeit.

On the Way to Utopia I

Birds: flying animals
Icarian flights
with bedraggled feathers
broken swoops
eyeless moreover
a bloody and panicked
flutter
in proper ornithological order
on the way to Utopia
which no one has reached alive
where only longing
winters

Only a poem preserves
what is already fading behind the horizon
something like true love and death
the two wings of life
moved by the last anguish
to a perfect
conclusion.

Unterwegs nach Utopia II

Auf der Flucht
vor dem Beton
geht es zu
wie im Märchen: Wo du
auch ankommst
er erwartet dich
grau und gründlich

Auf der Flucht findest du
vielleicht
einen grünen Fleck
am Ende
und stürzest selig
in die Halme
aus gefärbtem Glas.

On the Way to Utopia II

In flight
from the concrete
things happen
as in fairy tales: Wherever
you arrive
he is waiting for you
gray and grounded

On the flight you
may find
a green space
at the finish
and plunge blissful
into leaves
of colored glass.

Gedicht nach Benjamin

Der Feind der
zu siegen nicht aufgehört
zog die Toten aus ihren Gräbern
und maskiert ihr vertrautes Gebein
die ehrwürdigen Schädel
knüpft Fäden um ihre Gelenke
daß sie vorbildlich tanzen
und nie aus der Reihe
eine Sarabande trauriger als traurig
aus knöchernen Mündern
Wortbänder
als hätten sie je das gemeint
was sie jetzt sagen

Das soll ihr Nachleben sein

Der Feind aber der
zu siegen nicht aufhört
zieht die Toten aus ihren Gräbern
und tötet sie noch einmal.

Poem After Benjamin

The enemy who
does not cease to conquer
dragged the dead from their graves
and masked their entrusted bones
their honorable skulls
tied strings about their limbs
that they dance in a seemly fashion
and never out of step
a sarabande sadder than sad
from bony mouths
strings of words
as if they had always meant
what they now say

This should be their after-life

But the enemy who
does not cease to conquer
drags the dead from their graves
and kills them once again.

Biblische Geschichte II

Die Welt so ungetrübt
von Wirklichkeit wie hierzulande
wie es heißt und klingt und singt:
Kein Jammertal
vielmehr ein Paradies
geartet leidlos und gelitten
inmitten anderer Infernen: Nackt
steh ich da und du
nackt alle wenngleich nicht allen
sichtbar: Das ist Gesetz: Die Hände
ziemlich leer im Schweiße unsres Angesichts
höchste Moral durch Handbetrieb und
Naturalwirtschaft
Mundwerker überschäumend meist und kein Gedanke
bleibt geheim
es sei denn der unerforschlich ist für jeden
weil betrifft
Vergangenheit wie Gegenwart
so Zukunft nach sich zöge
was schon an Hiob statuiert: So also
desto lieber man
unter irdischen Gefährten
im prophezeiten Garten
dem einstmals ernst gemeinten
aus dem bizarrsten Buch der Bücher
schweigt.

Biblical History II

The world as untroubled
by reality as it is here
in the way it's named and sounds and sings:
No vale of woe
much rather Paradise
made painless and endured
in the midst of other infernos: Naked
I stand like you
naked to all if not visible
to all: This is law: Hands
mostly empty in the sweat of our brow
moral priority given handicraft and
organic husbandry
gift of gab foaming over and no thought
remaining secret
which cannot be fathomed by everyone
so that
the past drags the present
as well as future behind it
as was already decreed by Hiob: So that
living among mortal companions
in the prophesied garden
once taken seriously
in the most bizarre book of books
one would better
remain silent.

Venedig II

Nach dem Untergang Venedigs
werden sie sagen
(ihr wißt schon wer)
es hat nie eine Stadt
auf einer Lagune gegeben

Alles Erfindung

Und wer da Byzanz überfiel
das waren die Deutschen
wie von jeher
(Fränkische Ritter am Fallschirm)
Legenden beschreiben nur
einen erdachten Ort
Es ist bloß ein Begriff
für eine kanalisierte Anlage
doch nach einiger Zeit
am Horizont des Vergessens
tauchen die Kuppeln von San Marco auf
der Dogenpalast
die Piazetta mit den zwei Säulen trotzdem
und
die Gefängnisse füllen sich
mit Leuten die glauben
auf dem Canale Grande gefahren
zu sein.

Venice II

After its demise
they will say of Venice
(and you know who)
there never was a city
on the lagoon

All invention

And those who conquered Byzantium
those were the Germans
those earlier legends
(Frankish knights with parachutes)
describe only
an imagined place
It is only a scheme
for a canalization project
Nevertheless after some time
on the horizon of forgetfulness
San Marco's domes emerge
the Doge's Palace
the Piazza with two pillars
and
the prisons became filled
with people who believe
they have boated
on the Grand Canal.

Zur Archäologie unseres Verschüttetseins

Regen und wieder Regen
Krieg und wieder Krieg
Eins gnädig eins gnadenlos
einmal Natur aus erster einmal
aus zweiter Hand

Ein Zug fährt wieder
nach dreißigjährigen Kämpfen
die alte Strecke wie vordem
Ruinen verschwinden
aber mit ihnen die Welt
wie sie war

Nie nehmen wir wirklich Abschied
von unserer Vergangenheit
denn ehe wir zu ihr kommen
zerfiel sie
zu Staub und Asche irgendwo
als sie noch Gegenwart hieß

Auch würden wir gerne die Toten
einmal umarmen wären sie nicht schon
zu Worten verarbeitet worden
langen Gebinden aus Worten
die keine Gestalt mehr bezeugen

Hätten wir die Stimmen des Sterbens
festhalten können unser Ohr wäre kaum
so ertaubt vom Reden
Manchmal sind die Dinge
undurchdringlich manchmal glasklar
aber so wie Scherben
bevor man sich an ihnen verletzt
und verblutet.

On the Archaeology of our Interment

Rain and again rain
War and again war
One merciful one merciless
Nature on the one hand
man-made on the other

After thirty years of war
a train rides
the old track as before
ruins disappear
but with them the world
as it was

We never really take
leave of our past
because before we reach it
it disintegrates
into dust and ashes at those points
where one could still call it the present

We would gladly embrace
the dead were they not already
worked into words
long strings of words
no longer relevant to any shape

Could we have held on to
the voices of the dying our ear would not
be as deafened as with speech
At times things are
impenetrable sometimes clear as glass
but like splinters
before they wound us
and we bleed to death

Nachrichten aus der Provinz

Die ganz tiefen Zerstörungen
reichen bis unter die Oberfläche und bleiben
vorerst unsichtbar.
Eingesunken die Orte mancher Begegnung.
Inmitten der Ebenen stufige Brüche
unausgelotet. Hügelig wächst das Gras
aber es sind darunter eben Gräber.
Fassaden stehen noch doch
hinter den Gardinen schon nichts. Und
das Furnier klebt spekulativ
auf abwesendem Holz.
Wahr ist gar nichts mehr:
sobald du die Tür öffnest
befindest du dich nirgendwo. Schlage ein Buch auf
es enthält leere Worte.
Dein Bruder ist eine Hülle geworden
und geht so leicht umher
wie bestimmtes Papier. Wenn sich
die Früchte öffnen
fallen Welten zu Boden die nie blühen werden:
die Mühen der Zerstörung
haben den Kern erreicht der aussieht
wie ein Gehirn
winzig und zwischen Daumen und Zeigefinger
leicht zu zerbröckeln.

News from the Provinces

The really deep disturbances
reach the level of the surface and remain
invisible at first.
Sunken the places of many encounters.
In the midst of plains ungraded
gradual slopes. Grass grows in mounds
but what these cover are graves.
While facades remain
behind the curtains nothing. And
the veneer sticks speculatively
on wood that is not there.
Nothing is true any longer:
As soon as you open the door
you find yourself nowhere. Open a book
it contains empty words.
Your brother has become a shell
and moves around as lightly
as certain kinds of paper. When
fruits open
worlds fall to earth that will never bloom:
the disturbances
have reached and kernel that looks
like a brain
puny and easily crushed
between thumb and forefinger.

Bei Itzehoe

Fern dem Bereich
donnernder Genitive
amtlicher Vulkane Auswurf
darunter alles Leben
erstirbt

Jenseits und nördlich
meines verlassenen Daseins
also liegen tröstliche Flächen
zwischen Meer und Meer
Sumpf und Marsch
Nässe und Nichts

Jeder Schritt
führt in die Stille
durchsetzt von kleineren Städten
die sich ihr beugen

Hier
sind die bergenden Nebel zuhaus
und die Wikinger seit langem
archiviert

Near Itzehoe

Far from the nation
of thundering genitives
expressions of official vulcans
under which all life
is dying

Far away from and to the North
of my lost existence
comforting plains lie
between sea and sea
swamps and marsh
wetlands and nothing

Every step
leads to quiet
interspersed with small towns
that bow to it

Here
sheltering fogs are at home
and the Vikings gone into archives
long ago

Erinnern VIII

Wenn ich zurückdenke
sehe ich: Gestürzte Statuen
Manche blutet noch ein wenig
weil das authentischer ist
Prachtvolle Trümmer neugebaut
und wie antik
Windige Standarten
Legionen Schatten unterwegs
nach fünf Uhr nachmittags
zwischen zwei Arten Nichtsein

Ich sehe wieder Fliegen
in Auslagen verdorrt
überflüssige Symbole und trotzdem selten
von einer Verkäuferin entfernt

Ich sehe meine Jugend
Trunkenheit ohne Wein
zuerst dann mit: Mitleidend
blutend und vertrocknet später
Das Resümee: So ist Geschichte
denkt man und
zurück

Memory VIII

When I think back
I see: broken statues
Some still bleeding a little
that way more authentic
Magnificent ruins newly built
to simulate antiques
Standards in the wind
Shadows of legions on the road
after five o'clock in the afternoon
between two sorts of non-being

Again I see flies
dried up in the glass cases
superfluous symbols nevertheless rarely
removed by the shop-keeper

I see my youth
intoxication without wine
at first then with: Sympathy
bleeding and later dried up:
Resumé: This is history
one thinks thinking
back

Schlaf

Du träumst
den Traum des Jahrhunderts
sobald du
von amtlichen Schatten träumst
Nie zeigen sie ein Gesicht
sondern ihren Ausweis
und Gebärden
altbekannt von vielen früheren
Vergangenheiten
Sie zeigen dir
deine Angst und ihre Furcht
Pflöcke
durch Magenwand und Hoffnung
bis tief hinabgetrieben in den Boden
deines Landes

Da willst du fliehen
wenigstens erwachen aber wenn
das gelingt
umringen sie dein Bett seit langem
weil der Traum des Jahrhunderts
keiner ist

Sleep

You are dreaming
the dream of the century
when you dream
of administrative shadows
They never show a face
only the official mien
and gestures
familiar from many earlier
experiences
They show you
your dread and their fear
Stakes
through stomach wall and hope
driven deep into the ground
of your country

At that point you want to flee
at least wake up but
if you should
you'll find your bed has long been surrounded
because the dream of the century
is not one

Gespräche Abgeschiedener

Du arme geschundene Heimat
möchte ich sagen wollen
aber es gebricht mir an Stimme
unter uns gesagt
und zwischen Glas und Glas
Jahr um Jahr mehr

Irgendeinem System
wollten wir keinen Mann
und keinen Groschen geben
Das Leben währe zu kurz
war aber mit dieser Erkenntnis
auch schon zu Ende

So lüfte der Kellnerin den Rock:
Für ein paar Mark
findet sich überall Heimat
dunkel und wenig einladend
Jahr um Jahr weniger
wie Heimat meistens.

The Departed Speak

I could say
poor maligned homeland
but my voice would break
speaking amongst ourselves
and between glass and glass
year after year after year

We would not give
a human being and not one penny
for any system at all
Life is too short
and so finished
with this awareness

So raise the barmaid's skirts:
For a couple of mark
home can be found everywhere
dark and not very inviting
less and less year after year
as home usually is.

Vor der Sintflut

In den Abendbäumen
Gebilde aus purer Luft
langgezogen wie Rufe
aus weiter Ferne
und ich fragte mich
ob das der Abschied sei
oder sonst ein Zeichen
des Endes

Denn die Erde versinkt
hinter ihrem Horizont
nichts geht mehr auf
das ist klar
und es bleibt
ein fahriger Widerschein
von uns allen
noch eine Weile
bestehen

Before the Flood

In the evening trees
shapes of pure air
drawn out like calls
echoing from a distance
and I asked myself
was this farewell
or a similar sign
of the end

For the earth is sinking
behind the horizon
it will not rise again
so much is clear
there remains
a passing reflection
of all of us
that for a while
abides

Durchblick II

Im Fernrohr erscheinen fern
brennende Städte:
Feuer erlöschen Ruinen bleiben

Wer sonst trüge die Schuld
wenn nicht Prometheus
Unsere Streichholzschachtel
festverschlossen so haben wir
sie immer gehalten und können
jederzeit die Hölzchen
vollzählig vorweisen
zu unserer Entlastung.

Vista II

Distant burning cities
show in the telescope:
Fires extinguish ruins remain

Who else is to bear the blame
if not Prometheus
Our match box
is tightly shut as it
always has been
we can show you the full number
of matches at any time
to exonerate ourselves

Staatsbesuch

Stimmen und Maschinengeklapper
vom Ende der Welt her
in der Nähe aber Limousinen
geordnet hierarchisch und vorbei:
immer kleiner
durch die unwiderlegbare Perspektive
und
auf ein Schloß zu wie im Märchen

Schwarze Magie aus lackiertem Blech
aus feierlichem Anzug und Aufzug
ein Schauspiel
als blicke man in sehr ferne Vergangenheit
wo die Menschen nicht wissen
daß sie Hintergrund sind
und noch hoffen

Aber die Geschichte
bringt nichts zurück obwohl sie alles
unsäuberlich wiederholt

State Visits

Voices and the chatter of machines
coming from the end of the world
but nearby limousines
hierarchically ordered moving past
growing ever smaller
in unchanging perspective
towards
a castle in a fairy tale

Black magic out of polished metal
out of festive dress and parade
a piece of theatre
as if one were looking into the distant past
where the people did not realize
they were merely background
and continued hoping

But history
brings nothing back although what it repeats
returns dirtied

Bürogebet

Leicht zusammengeheftet
mit einer gebrechlichen Klammer
die mich vor manchem bewahrt
das ich nur ahne und nicht sage:
Denn viele
fielen einfach auseinander
wortreich und darum
hoffnungslos

Ihre Teile treiben umher

Hier ein Stück gekniffter Charakter
Ein Fetzen verlorener Mut
Etwas verblichene Liebe
Ein trostloser Anblick

Irgendwem aus der Hand gerutscht
einem plötzlich verstorbenen
Vorsteher
den man versehentlich
für Gott halten könnte

Bewahr mich davor

Office Prayer

Loosely bound
with a fragile clip
which has saved me from much
I only suspect and will not say:
Because many
simply fall apart
rich in words and therefore
hopeless

Their parts passing here and there

Here a piece of pinched character
a rag-tag of lost courage
A somewhat paled love
A disconsolate look

Slipped out of someone's grasp
sudden death
of a surrogate
one could for the time being
take for God

Preserve me from that

Forschungsauftrag

Heute hat das Glück
keine Namen mehr
Es hat sein Ansehen
verloren
sein Aussehen Die Kugel
Das Füllhorn Das Kleeblatt

Wer es sucht
findet an seiner Stelle
nichts
eine Lücke im Befinden
im Mauerwerk der Welt
einen Riß

jenseits dessen vielleicht
Angstlosigkeit anfängt

Research Project

Today there is no name
for luck any longer
It has lost
its outline
its appearance The Globe
The horn of plenty The clover leaf

Instead we find
Nothing
in our search for it
a hiatus in existence
a breach
in the brickwork of the world

perhaps for that reason
fearlessness may now begin

Kein Sommer Keine Schonzeit

Vorm Fenster mal Nebel mal Polizisten
die Gegend erblaßt
die Gegend verliert und geht uns verloren
die Natur versteckt sich natürlich
in Zweideutigkeit
Hingegen wir werden
amtlicherseits scharf umrissen
und bilden ein Wunschbild
Jagdzauber
in den geheimen Akten: Da stehen wir
fest wie in Wirklichkeit nie
weil Akten und Polizei wirklicher sind
als der tägliche Ephemeride
in deinem und meinem Spiegel
verstört vom Schlaf
keine Vollendung träumend
nichts träumend außer
im Wort zu bleiben: Aber das
verfärbt sich schon selber
und verdorrt mit der Zeit
fällt und versinkt
in Nebel und Akten
unauferstehbar.

No Summer No Closed Season

At the window sometimes fog sometimes policemen
the neighborhood pales
the neighborhood loses and is lost to us
naturally nature hides itself
in ambivalence
while we on the other hand
are sharply circumscribed
and form a dream image:
Magic of the hunt
in secret files: There we stand
firm as never in reality—
where documents and the police are more real
than the daily ephemeral being
in your mirror and mine
disturbed in sleep
dreaming of no fulfillment
dreaming nothing but
to remain on paper: But that
is already discoloring
and in time decays
falls and sinks
into fog and documents
not to be resurrected.

Eingeschriebene Antwort

In manchen Gegenden wie meiner
herrscht stumpfe Stille
wo wer von der Post zehrt
wie die Fliege von winzigen Resten
täglich alt wird und es nicht merkt

Die Entfernung und die Blätter im Frühjahr
mildern die Leiden
Denn so unvorstellbar ist die Welt
geworden so gänzlich dahin
hinter dem blechernen Kasten
hinter dem Drahtzaun
der Mauer der Blende den Reden
hinter dem oberirdischen Rohr
der Fernheizung olivfarben und leblos
daß man nicht mehr
an sie zu glauben vermag
Selbst die Versprechen der Regierungen
hier und da
werden zu nichts noch bevor
der Briefträger sie in den Spalt
pressen kann
in den Ausschnitt
der das Universum geometrisch
begrenzt.

Registered Letter

In many neighborhoods like mine
there is a dull silence
where those feeding on the mail
like the fly on minute remains
grow older daily without noticing it

Distance and the leaves in spring
soften sorrow for
the world has become so
unimaginable so wholly gone
behind the metal box
behind the barbed wire
the wall the blinds the speeches
behind the steam pipes
running above ground olive and lifeless
that one can no longer
trust in it
The promises of governments themselves
here and there
come to nothing even before
the postman can push them
through the slot
in the cut-out
that geometrically borders
the universe.

Deutsche Elegie

Ein guter Deutscher und noch
einer und noch
weiß nicht was geschehen ist
was geschieht und geschehen wird
Abwesend gewesen sein und bleiben
geistig oder sonstwie ideal
verstopften Ohres eh
die Schüsse fielen oder bloß
die ihnen vorausgesandten Worte
oder das Signal zum Weghören alle mal

Keine geographische Begrenzung

trotz geteilter Himmel
Blindheit Taubheit Stummheit
wie von heiligen Makaken jener
und der und dieser noch
befehlsgemäß erstarrt
zu Bronze die später immer
sich als Gips erweist.

German Elegy

A good German and still
another and still
does not know what happened
what happens and will happen
Having been absent and remaining
spiritually or otherwise ideally so
ears stopped up before
the shots rang out or were these
words sent out ahead of them
or the signal to listen absent at all times

No geographical limits

despite divided skies
Blindness Deafness Dumbness
as if by the command
of the sacred macaca this one and
he and that one were frozen
in bronze that later turned out
to be plaster

Neues von den Antipoden

Keine Zuflucht
bieten Dschungel noch Städte
und das geheime System
der Abwasserkanäle nicht
auf Dauer

Die Gesichter Grimassen
kläglich und beiläufig
bevor der Schuß fällt
der sie für immer entspannt

Jede Revolution
bade im Blut heißt es
ihrer Reinheit wegen
Aber wenn sie siegt
sind die Überlebenden
überflüssig

wie verdorrte Blumen
auf dem Schreibtisch
der Macht

News from the Antipodes

Neither jungle nor cities
offer refuge
and the secret sewer
system not made
for a long stay

Faces grimace
piteously for the present
before the shot hits
that will forever release them

Every revolution
its own blood-bath it is said
for the sake of its purity
but after victory
the survivors become
superfluous

like wilted flowers
on the desks of
power

Berlin

Da ist nichts mehr
zu beschreiben. Stattdessen
verhöhnt Beton alles Eingedenken
und verschachtelt Bewohner für immer.
Fort die unergründlichen Labyrinthe
klägliche Zimmer düstere Läden
und das allabendliche Sanssouci
betäubender Kneipen
der glanzvolle Ernst der Seifengeschäfte
voll Buntheit und Bürsten gebunden
von wirklich Blinden und alte Frauen
von Fenstern gerahmt
bürgten für Dauer und Fortbestand.
Geduldig und schweigend
korrodierte in Fabrikshöfen die Zeit:
eine lebendige Weise von Tod
und im Dunkel
einer schon bald vergessenen Toreinfahrt
lauerte das Glück ohne Namen:

Jetzt ist alles benannt und vermessen
abgeheftet und niedergerissen
und nichts mehr da
zum Beschreiben.

Berlin

There is nothing left
to describe. Instead
concrete mocks all remembrance
and boxes inmates for evermore.
Gone the impenetrable labyrinths
of miserable rooms and gloomy shops
and the routine evening Sans Souci
of ear deafening taverns
the bright seriousness of bathroom shops
full of color and brushes tied
by the truly blind and old ladies
framed in the windows
attesting to enduring qualities.
Patiently silently
time corroded in factory yards:
a living kind of death
while in the dark
of an almost forgotten gateway
a nameless kind of luck lurked:

Now everything is named and measured
torn away and broken down
and there is nothing left
to describe.

Regloser Augenblick

Eigentlich
keine Ahnungen. Ich stehe
am Fenster und sehe hinaus
aber
es ist nichts zu sehen. Nichts
Schlimmes eigentlich. Es regnet nicht
und es friert nicht
kein Wind keine Sonne keine Leute kein Auto
Nur ein nackter leerer Moment
Jede Bedeutung verflüchtigt
verflogen der ehmals mildernde Dunst
Rundum mißratene Schicksale
geschichtsgleich: Am Fenster stehen
und hinaussehen und nichts erwarten
Alle zehn Jahre ein Blick
in die Zeitung reicht aus
Schleichendes Verhängnis: Schon
reden sie wieder von ihren Idealen

Wenn ich ein Baum wäre
ich stünde jetzt unter Schutz
wie die Tannen die mir gehören
aber ich gehöre niemand
und stehe daher nicht unter Schutz
sondern am Fenster
und sehe hinaus

Motionless Moment

Actually
no presentiments. I'm standing
at the window looking out
but
there is nothing to see. Nothing
bad really. It's not raining
and it's not freezing
no wind no sun no people no car
Only a naked empty moment
Every significance fled
the erstwhile softening mist dispersed
Round about failed destinies
like history: standing at the window
looking out and expecting nothing
Every ten years a glance
into the paper suffices
Creeping disaster: They're
already speaking of their ideals again

If I were a tree
I would now be protected
like the fir trees that belong to me
but I belong to no one
and therefore am not protected
but at the window
looking out

Abtötungsverfahren

Ein Blick in die Zeitung
und einer ins Leben
Ein Gespräch mit den Stummen
und eine Rede von Tauben
Ein Entfalten der Flügel
und die Aussicht in Mündungen
Ein Versuch die Hand auszustrecken
und das Berühren von Eisen
Eine Tüte voll Angst
für das Dasein als Körper
gründlich einverleibt
der Leichengemeinschaft

Erst ein Ausflug ins Jenseits
dann eine Rückkehr ins Nichts.

Mortification Acts

A glance into the paper
and one into life
A talk with the dumb
and a speech about pigeons
An unfolding of wings
and the view into muzzles
An attempt to reach out a hand
and the touch of iron
A bag full of fear
for existence as a body
fully incorporated
into the society of corpses

First a flight into the beyond
and then a return into nothingness.

Andromeda Out of Season

Departure, departure.

All night long the take-off and flight to the blinking light-points, to the settlement planets in the Cassiopeia constellation. Zero hour on the dot the painted torso of a female announcer opens bright red lips, and after announcements of weather conditions, humidity and some inter-planetary news, says: "It is zero o'clock." She adds the date in a restrained whisper and closes with a good-night smile and a reference to the TV transmission of today's flight which will follow.

Departure flight: Not many are left who still watch their sets for the take-off. For many years now it has grown too familiar. Always the same picture: Hundreds of people streaming out of a flat-roofed central station. They have been chosen for the ride to these planets which physically resemble the earth but where there is neither a lack of food nor an unequal distribution of this lack. We see them file into long single lines moving towards gigantic rocket ships, boarding them with one last backward wave, smiling greetings into the camera, suitcase in one hand, cap held high in the other, and then to disappear, all of them, all into these flightworthy machines.

Sitting in our living room chair we can see that a camera has been set up at some distance where it will be protected from the pressure waves of the take-off procedure. This camera now transmits the whole of the Departure Area emptied of humans, into the midnight chambers of those who, for whatever reason, and careless of their energy supply, are avoiding their beds.

A flowery dimpled smile: This is Friday, February 25, zero o'clock. We are transmitting Flight Number Eight thousand five hundred and sixty-six and bid all planetarians good night. White fire shoots out of the blunt end of the take-off planes: one after another rises heavily from the scaffold, material and machinery seemingly hesitant: should they really start out on this long journey? Suddenly these booming bodies come to a decision: the ascent quickens, grows fast, faster, the eye of the camera weaving along with it: finally a steady upward rise into the prospective heavens, into the unbelievable stage of world theater: always the same series of events of which most viewers have already tired for it has been repeated night after night for half a decade. It has grown boring. Sometimes the news broadcasts report on the day's doings on Uranus or Neptune; these are of small technical interest and not shown in color so that it is hard to make out details. People harvest fruit from trees, drive in cars, sit in front of dwelling spheres, and, although details are neither clear nor identifiable, seem well-nourished and carefree in contrast to the terrestrial population which must survive on subsistence rations. Here, thanks to the carelessness of preceding generations there is not enough for all so that emigration has become the rule, nightly flights at zero hour. Those who received the green boarding card in the mail must report at the Departure Area; these are the happy people who will soon partake of the fleshpots of the galaxy.

Time for bed, after undressing with the fewest possible motions to minimize caloric expenditure. Lying there one can still feel the jet flames flicker behind closed lids, earth-directed torches of this Promethean undertaking. If one could only fly along. No more talk about food, no more secret leafing through yellowed cook books. No more hopelessly greedy gaze at the last remaining birds, magpie or crow, which have been placed under protective custody that in no way prevents them from dying out (to be honest, from being eaten). But volunteers are not accepted!

One must show the green card, otherwise the universe, of which there is indeed very little knowledge, remains closed. Yes, the further the flights, the less is known. As if the price of extending space is a restriction in the general ability to learn anything of this newly gained space beyond the scientific: as knowledge broadens it levels. So one lies in bed and knows that one knows much too much. And that it profits nothing. It neither satisfies, nor strengthens, nor pacifies, nor consoles: the 30th century, resting in its apogee, permits a view of itself but remains silent: a monolith of a continuous and measurable passage in time.

Departure, departure.

Sleepless at the zero hour, facing the ultra short-wave female with her swollen bursting lips: Tuesday, the 10th of April, zero hour—we are transmitting Flight number. . . . Hordes are lining up as directed by the soft loudspeaker voice.

Boarding.

Now as the count-down begins, the colors suddenly separate, the spectrum spreads into a rainbow behind the glass from which an invisible soft voice says: technical difficulties, please stand by. And immediately the colors fuse again. Flames shoot out from the space ships, released they rise slowly at first, then more quickly, up to the Northern ecliptic: stars with ultra brightness dissolve quickly and disappear between Andromeda Fish and Pegasus Swan. Blinking spots signal star constellations. All these once had to be painfully memorized in the classroom because to children these haphazardly glowing spots never looked like Egyptian princesses, winged horse or other inhabitants of sea or sky.

But now these constellations are pictured on the screen; they blink, twinkle, the program is finished, bed is waiting, we undress slowly and only when we are under the covers do we suddenly realize, with something almost like a chill, the wondrous thing we have seen: today, the 10th of April, zero hour, Andromeda Fish and Pegasus Swan aren't even in the skies!

With practiced quiet hand motions the covers are removed and we go to the window: a fact—outside above the rooftops there is an entirely different sky than the one we saw transmitted earlier. While shivering, we reflect. Next evening palpitations in front of the screen. The pulse quickens as the sound comes over: "zero hour . . ." and "departure. . . ." On the screen old men bent over their stick are dragging their baggage, white haired old ladies with crippled fingers wave at the camera, their eyes glowing with hope and greed for life. Among the travellers young people move with spirited laughter, full toothed mouths, hungry for the Garden of Eden on the other side of earthly want where a better life is waiting. And so the travellers file towards the jets, moved along by the friendly announcements from the public address system in the control tower.

Finally the last steel door closes on the last passenger. For a moment the picture disappears. But quickly another will appear on the screen: that of the Departure Area as seen from the hidden camera. Soon we shall have it together with the night sky, marine blue today and starry, and there, the anxiously awaited view of the concrete surface, and at its limits on the horizon, the black space with its constellations, nebula and planets, conforming to the seasons and the time. We can breathe again.

But something of yesterday's anxiety remains: why did another sky cover the Departure Area yesterday: a thorn, even when on the following nights everything appears true to form. The feeling lurks, cannot be repressed: At a warm, welcoming house a hand opens the door behind which there waits an unlit abyss, an unknown darkness, instead of the expected guest room. Even after the door closes never to be re-opened, an unstilled restlessness drags at our heels, until we dare speak of it, our tone ironic and self-mocking: Just imagine, recently, at one of the departures, the November sky appeared in the middle of April! I swear to you, there was Andromeda! Just as if somebody had placed the wrong film in the projector. . . .

Once the secret shapeless doubt has been expressed, the psyche feels relief from its oppression. The anxiety disappears once it is made public. And when three days after we have purged ourselves in the company of our friends, we stand in the lobby at the mailboxes and find the desired green card ordering our departure, we are quite certain that we dreamed this extraordinary appearance of Andromeda.

III
In the Poem's Net

Memory of Scheria

Once more to regain this moment: on these porous cliffs, warmed by the sun, surrounded by water clear to the bottom where shadowy organisms flit, dumb messengers of a past far beyond our own, the blessed mid-day peace punctuated by a lone cicada, sheltered by bushes, laurel or oleander, low-growing pines with long needles: here to come to self-awareness. Here your foot, your hand, belly and limb, joint and hair, for a short while in steady state: so that you sense them once more and again. He who can regain this moment, he would be privy to bliss, and one other than that of cliff, of water, light and nothingness.

Nausikaa I

Fand mich. Schickte fort
die Freundinnen.
Unter Sonnengeißeln, unter dem Gebüsch
am Strande,
unter Stöhnen, Stammeln wirrer Worte,
löste sich die ganze Insel
der Phaiaken
auf in Lust, in Leiblichkeit,
bis am Ende nach dem Ende
nur ihr Körperabdruck blieb im Sand
zurück: größte Kostbarkeit,
die ich je zurückgelassen, und ihr wißt:
selten nur ließ was zurück
Odysseus,
außer seinem Samen, voller Zweifel
an irgendeine Wiederkehr
irgendeines Augenblickes.

Nausicaa I

Found me. Sent away
the girl companions.
Under the scorching sun, under the brush
at the shore,
under moaning, mumbling wild chaotic words
the whole island of the Phaeacians
dissolved
in lust, in fleshly joys
until in the end after the end
only her body's imprint was left in the
sand: the most precious
thing I ever left behind, and you know:
rarely was anything left behind by
Odysseus
besides his seed, doubtful
of any possible return
at any time at all.

Nausikaa II

Man weiß nicht, wo man landet.
Man weiß nur: hier
hört die Sonne nie zu scheinen auf.
Leichter Wellenschlag
an den zarten Sand bleichen Strandes:
Insel-Rhythmus.

Nackt kommt dem Ankömmling
das andere Geschlecht entgegen:
phallisches Blühen,
gefördert von der Hitze
des Mittags.

Leben ist und Tod ist
ganz einfach: ein zahnloses Dahocken
zum Schluß, den Blick
aufs reglose Meer, den Rücken
am rissigen Fels, kein Erwarten mehr,
kein Hoffen: letzte Erkenntnis,
daß des
vorübergegangenen Aufenthaltes Ort
kein anderer gewesen als
Scheria.

Nausicaa II

One doesn't know where one has landed.
One knows only: here
the sun never fails to shine.
Soft rush of waves
on the gentle sand of the pale shore:
island rhythm.

Naked the other sex
approaches the new arrivals:
phallic flowering
the mid-day heat
generates.

Life is and death is
very simple: a toothless cowering
at the end, the eye
on the motionless sea, the back
towards the rough cliffs, no more expectations,
no hope: a final recognition
that the place lost in passage
was no other than
Scheria.

Orpheus I

Nicht umdrehen.
Der Sänger drehe sich besser nicht um.
Ein leichter Schritt, ein schleichendes
Schreiten, ein feines Getrappel,
pulsjagendes Stöckeln: sie
folgt mir schon, folgt meinem Lied,
folgsam Trochäen und Jamben: Schreiten
heraus aus verstorbenem Gestern wir beide:
Hinter der Kunst kommt
die Zukunft voran.

Der Sänger drehe sich besser nicht um.

Orpheus I

Don't turn around.
The singer better not turn around.
A soft step, a slinking
glide, a fine tripping,
a pulse-racing clatter: she'll
follow me, follow my song,
compliant to trochee and iamb: marching
out from dead yesterdays the two of us:
Behind art
the future advances.

The singer better not turn around.

Orpheus II

Unverhofft beschworene Erscheinung
tritt aus dem ruhlosen Tartarus
meines Hirns,
so tritt aus Fels die Substanz:
Eurydike,
hervorgelockt von tränenseligen Schlagern,
dem Anhauch nächtiger Städte vielleicht,
vielleicht vom löblichen Schnaps
schmerzlich und schmählich und wirst
genauer besehn und bei Licht
zunichte:

Abwesend gelebt in mir lange Zeit,
bevor deiner gedacht ward,
gebrechlicher Schatten,
verdampfst du jetzt auf dem Gestein
menschlichen Erinnerns.

Orpheus II

Unexpected conjured appearance
sprung from the restless Tartarus
of my brain
so from stone the substance:
Euridice
lured here by bliss of tearful pop tunes,
the night-time breath of cities perhaps,
perhaps by whiskey's solace
painful and paltry and soon
seen more clearly and in the light
wiped out:

Absently alive within me a long time,
before I brought you to mind,
fragile shadow,
now to evaporate on the stone
of human memory.

Orpheus III

War es denn recht,
die bereits selig versunken
in die Anonymität allgemeiner Jenseitigkeit
zurückführen zu wollen
in Abgründe schmerzbringenden Fleisches,
in die Langweile abstumpfender Zellen
und hin zu gewisser Enttäuschung: Mehltau
aus zerriebener Hoffnung,
der alles Blühen befällt.

Nichts ist so unwiederholbar wie Glück.

Ich sah schon
künftiger Tage Lawinen aus Gleichgültigkeit,
wachsende Schichten von Fremdheit und Staub
uns beide verschütten, bevor ich darum
Dich ansah:
berühmter falsch gedeuteter Augen-Blick,
unvergeßlich und fragend:
War es denn recht?

Orpheus III

And was it right
the wish to lead her
already blissful sunken
in the general anonymity of the world beyond
back to the abysmal sorrows of the flesh,
from the boredom of neutralized cells
back to certain frustration: the meal
composed of grated hopes,
the fate of every blossom.

Nothing is as irretrievable as happiness.

I could already see
an avalanche of indifference in the future,
layers of estrangement and dust developing
destroying us both, before I turned
to look at you:
famous moment falsely interpreted,
never to be forgotten, asking:
was it right?

Orpheus VI

Da erhält jeder seinen Lohn
wenn der Plattenspieler läuft
im Keller eines Hauses
in Berlin und anderswo:
da erhält und empfindet jeder
was ihm gebührt

wenn nicht beim ersten Male
dann beim zweiten oder dritten
oder fünfzigsten:
und wird erlöst von seinen Leiden
von Zahnschmerz und Weltschmerz
vom Mangel an Paris Rom London

und Gerechtigkeit und
eigenem Leben

erlöst für drei Minuten
durch Frank Sinatra oder Nat King Cole
oder wie auch immer sich
heut nennen mag
der zerfleischte Sänger
der niemals stirbt
der thrakische.

Orpheus VI

When the record player spins
in the basement room of a house
in Berlin or elsewhere:
there each one takes his reward
each one takes and senses
what is due him

when not the first time
the second or the third
or fiftieth:
and is released from pain
from toothache and Weltschmerz
from lack of Paris Rome London

and justice and
his own life

released for three minutes
by Frank Sinatra or Nat King Cole
or however he may
be called today
the incorporated singer
who will never die
the Thracian.

Gedicht zum Gedicht

Mehr als ein Gedicht
ist beispielsweise: Kein Gedicht,
denn das Nichtgedicht lebt
als sanfte Lauheit der Inspiration:
Umweltgefühl
des Tropfens im Wasser.
Der Leib fühlt sich geborgen.
Das Herz fühlt nichts.
Die Waage ist ausgeglichen.
Das Lot hängt still.

Gedicht ist Zustand,
den das Gedicht zerstört,
indem es
aus sich selber hervortritt.

Poem to a Poem

More than a poem
would be, for example: no poem,
because the no-poem lives
as gentle spawn of inspiration:
sensibility towards what surrounds
the drop in water.
The body feels protected.
The heart nothing.
The scale is balanced
the plumb-line still.

Poem is a condition
which the poem destroys
as it
moves out of itself.

Erscheinung, unerwartet

Ein Gedicht hat in mir gewartet
lange Zeit
ohne sich bemerkbar zu machen
ein geduldiger Ausbrecher der heimlich
die Gitter durchfeilt

Das Ei der großen Meeresschildkröte
reift so verborgen im Sand

Ein Gedicht hat sich auf seine Stunde bereitet
lange Zeit
um am 22. Juli 1972 14.25 Uhr selber
in die Zeitlichkeit zu schlüpfen
zu meinem Staunen
aus einem Irgendwoher
dessen ich nie einsichtig wurde

Eine innere Verfaltung scheint es
etwas wie das dem die Kristalle entwachsen
und dann zaghaft birst

Jene alte Wunde vermutlich
die gereizt nach außen durchbricht und
aufblüht
plötzlich und nach langer Zeit.

Appearance Unexpected

A poem has waited in me
for some time
not calling attention to itself
a patient jail-breaker secretly
filing bars

The egg of the giant sea turtle
matures in the sand like that

A poem has readied itself for its hour
for some time
and on July 22, 1972, 2:25 A.M.
slipped into temporality
to my surprise
coming from nowhere at all
completely unsuspected

Like an interior fold
something like a crystalline growth
that hesitantly breaks

Possibly that old wound
that irritated breaks through the surface
and blossoms
suddenly and after a long time.

Nachgedicht

Sobald die Erde abgefressen ist
von der Säure der Luft
vom Hunger der Menschen
tritt allerorts Fels vor
verwittertes Gestein oder Marmor
Geröll Kiesel Kalk und Karst:
Höhlen
verblieben und in ihren
unbeschrittenen Tiefen taube Wörter
alte vergessene Wörter
blinde Wörter
reglos
ungelesen.

Da liegt ihr also
und wenn der Boden schüttert
wie unter einem Tritt
beginnt ihr hinzukriechen
dem Nichtvorhandenen und Nichtgekommenen
entgegen: Euch mitzuteilen: wegzugeben:
Bettler.

Latterday Poem

As soon as the earth is eaten up
by acid in the air
the hunger of people
all kinds of crags will appear
weathered stone or marble
rubble, gravel, chalk, lime
Hollows
remain and in their
untrodden depths deaf words
old forgotten words
blind words
unmoved
unread.

So there you lie
and when the ground shakes
as if under a footstep
you begin to creep
towards the not-yet-present not-yet-arrived:
to share yourselves: give yourselves away:
Beggars.

So soll es sein

Zwecklos und sinnvoll
soll es sein
zwecklos und sinnvoll
soll es auftauchen aus dem Schlamm
daraus die Ziegel der großen Paläste
entstehen um wieder zu Schlamm zu zerfallen
eines sehr schönen Tages

zwecklos und sinnvoll
soll es sein
was für ein unziemliches Werk
wäre das
zur Unterdrückung nicht brauchbar
von Unterdrückung nicht widerlegbar
zwecklos also
sinnvoll also

wie das Gedicht.

So It Should Be

Purposeless and meaningful
so it should be
purposeless and meaningful
it should rise from the mud
from which the great palaces
were created in order to sink back into mud
one very fine day

purposeless and meaningful
so it should be
what an unsuitable work
that would be
not to be used for oppression
not to be put down by oppression
purposeless therefore
meaningful therefore

like a poem.

Im Netz des Gedichtes

fängt sich manchmal
etwas Wirklichkeit
bis zur Unkenntlichkeit
eingesponnen
blutlos

Im Bild des bekannten
Flechtwerks
das jeden Durchblick erlaubt
lauert die beiläufige Bestie
Analogie

die alles Einmalige sofort
verschlingt

In the Poem's Net

some reality
is sometimes caught
entangled
beyond recognition
bloodless

In the picture of the familiar
network
which allows for every kind of view
there lurks the parenthetical beast:
analogy

which immediately swallows everything
unique.

Gedicht

Immer verweigert sich
das erste Wort und sträubt sich
Immer ist es das zweite
das sich hervortut: das schwächere.
Es hat einen Sprung
das hört man am Klang

Das erste Wort wäre so
wie wenn bei Sonnenaufgang
das Licht
durch einen langen steinernen Gang
zum ersten Mal
in eine ferne erdbedeckte Kammer
fiele und sie erhellte

Aber immer drängt sich
das falsche Wort vor und
das Innerste der Welt
bleibt dunkel
weiterhin.

Poem

It is always the first word
that hesitates and resists
it is always the second
that pushes forward: the weaker.
It has a spring
one can hear in the tone.

The first word would be
as if at sunrise
the light
would come through a long stone passage
to brighten
for the first time a distant
earth covered chamber

But the spurious word
always presses forward and
the center of the world
continues
to stay dark.

Fiktion

Es gibt eine Ewigkeit
wie ich sie mir vorstelle
als fortgesetzte Bewegung
als Tanz
zu einem alten Schlager im Halbdunkel
eines ganz verbrauchten Lokales
im Duft von Schweiß und Puder
einer Partnerin
fremder und doch inniger Körper
umarmt in immergleicher Melodie
langsamer Walzer vielleicht
etwas schwungvoll Schleppendes
nur daß manchmal eine versteckte Stimme
sänge: Dream a little dream of me
und sich unsere Lippen küßten
so als wären sie
von uns selber Jahrtausende fern
unter sonst ganz gewöhnlichen Lampen
die mein Auge blenden.

Fiction

The way I picture
eternity is
as continuous movement
like dance
to an old pop tune in the dim light
of a worn out dance hall
with the sweat and powder scent
of my partner
foreign yet intimate bodies
embraced in an everlasting melody
possibly a slow waltz
sometimes a dragging swing
at times a hidden voice
singing: *Dream a little dream of me*
with our lips kissing
as if they were
thousands of years removed from us
beneath otherwise very ordinary lights
that blind my eyes

1974

Ein Gedicht mit dem Titel
»Neunzehnhundertvierundsiebzig«
wäre kein langes Gedicht
käme es zu einem wie es zu einem
geringfügigen Unfall im Haushalt kommt

Ach stets ereignen sich unversehens
Gedichte deren Inhalt doch ständig
dreihundertfünfundsechzig Tage überschreitet
pendelnd zwischen
Kindheit und Blindheit
des Augenblicks

Ein Gedicht unter einer Jahreszahl
enthielte zumindest zwölf Monate
Frühling Sommer Herbst und Winter
Fortschritt Frühstück Abendbrot
Folter Mord und Totschlag
und eine Überbelastung der Herzkranzgefäße
in Erwartung der Ausreiseerlaubnis
Besuche von Freunden wie Feinden
Nahost und Nahwest im täglichen Fernsehen
Schlaf und Beischlaf
und davor und danach jene
nie ruhende Frage

Ist es nicht richtiger ganz und gar
frei zu sein
keinem verbunden keinen Menschen
keiner Sache
einzig noch dem Gedicht

und später im Kalender zwischen Kiel
und München und Recklinghausen
zwischen Orten
denen die Eile das Aussehen raubt

1974

A poem with the title
"Nineteenhundredandseventyfour"
would not be a long poem
should it come upon one the way
a minor accident happens in the home

Oh unplanned poems are always
happenings whose contents
swinging between
innocence and the blindness
of the moment
transcend threehundredandsixtyfive days

A poem situated beneath a number of a year
would hold at least twelve months
spring summer fall and winter
progress breakfast supper
torturous murder and death blow
an overload of the heart's circulatory system
in the wait for the emigration permit
visits of friends as well as enemies
near-East and near-West on the daily TV
sleep and sleeping with
and before and afterwards that
never ending question

Isn't it better to be
altogether free
bound to no one no man
no thing

ein hastiges Hin und Her
um da und dort vor verschiedenen Leuteligkeiten
zu verlesen
was wie Frühling Sommer Herbst
und Winter klingt
was klingt wie Folter Mord und Totschlag
wie: Hier ist ein Anlaß
zur Selbstdiagnose jenes heillosen Leidens
das manchmal zum Leben führt

wie ein Gedicht also
das nicht mehr ist als ein Gedicht.

solely only to the poem
and later in the calendar between Kiel
and Munich and Recklingshausen
between places
towards which the rush robs the view
a hasty back and forth
for readings before various kinds of people
here and there
what sounds like spring summer
fall and winter
what sounds like torturous murder and death blow
like: Here is a situation
for self diagnosis of that incurable pain
that sometimes leads to life

that is like a poem
which is no more than a poem.

Spur

So fremde Spur ist Wort
um Wort: Von Satz zu Satz.
Man schreibt sich immer weiter fort
und bleibt dabei am selben Platz.

Maschinenlärm und Todesschreie
der kalte Ton von ferneher:
Syntaktisch bildet sich die Reihe
in der du stehst: Ein Irgendwer.

Ein Tastendruck: Du bist gewesen.
Die Faust geballt: sie hält nichts fest.
Am Anfang war das Wort zu lesen:
Erinnern hieß es. Nicht: Vergeßt.

Trace

Such a strange track the word
to a word: from phrase to phrase
one writes on always drawing further outward
only to remain fixed in place.

Machine screech and mortal cries
the cold tone from a distant place
syntactic build-up of the series
in which you stand: An any-face.

A pressure touch: You once have been
The fist is balled: nothing is kept
Originally the word was written:
It read remember. Not: forget.

Schicksal des Gedichts

Zum Lügen gezwungen
erbleicht das Gedicht
Es erstarrt und kann
sich und nichts mehr rühren

Zum Lobe
des Martyriums und des Verbrechens
spricht es feierlich und fürchterlich
die Absicht amtlicher Akteure aus

Eingefangen und der Freiheit beraubt
front es
im Steinbruch verhärterter Ideen
schleppt alle großen Worte herbei
aus denen Gefängnisse
für Gedanken entstehen

Und selbst wenn es selber
ausbricht und aufschreit
in der Benennung der Mörder
erstirbt das Gedicht im Gedicht
rettungslos

Poem's Destiny

Forced to lie
the poem pales
It freezes and can no longer
move itself or anything

In praise of
martyrdom and criminal acts
it makes festive and frightful pronouncements
designed for official actors

Imprisoned and robbed of freedom
it fronts
as quarry of hardened ideas
drags all the grand words along
from which the prisons
for thought are created

And even when it itself
breaks out and cries out
in naming the murderer
the poem dies in the poem
beyond salvation

Theatrum Mundi

Täglich treibt Ophelia
an dir vorbei. Ein Hamlet
nach dem anderen verblutet
Der Rest ist schlimmer
als Schweigen
weil Heuchelei. Du triffst sie täglich
Bruder deine Brüder
aus der Klassik und Fausti Wehklag
enthält die alten neuen Leiden
von einem der sich verkauft hat.
Der weise Nathan
hat seine Pflicht und Schuldigkeit
getan und ist verbrannt.
Macht nichts! das Publikum
erfindet selbst sich neue Juden.
Nur du und ich
beschmutzt von Furcht und Mitleid
aller Dramen
erfahren nichts als daß
wir die Komparsen sind
jenseits der Worte
die uns keiner gab.

Theatrum Mundi

Ophelia daily
passes by your side. One Hamlet
after another bleeds to death.
As for the rest it is worse
than silence
because hypocrisy. You meet it daily
Brother your brothers
in the classics with the Faustian cry of woe
inherited the old new sorrows
from one who sold himself.
Wise Nathan
did his duty paid his debt
and then was burned.
No matter! The public
will find itself new Jews.
Only you and I
smudged with the drama's
fear and pity
learn nothing but
that we are the mutes
alongside words
that nobody dealt us.

Die Gedichte

Ziemlich schwebende Gebilde

aber gleichen sie nicht Hohn
über soviel Elend und Tötungen
über dem stillen Sterben
das alle Welt ergreift
Urwälder Einwohner Elefanten
Schwärme im Meer
und in der Luft und sogar
die Luft selber
Kennzeichnendes Spiel
steigender und fallender Worte
Kadenzen
von denen kein Armer reich
kein Reicher klüger
kein Kluger
zum rechten Handeln befähigt wird

Schwebende Gebilde wie Rauch
ein Spiel wie von Feuer
während darunter
das Holz sich sinnlos verzehrt.

The Poems

Hovering weaving images

but do they not seem derisive
above so much misery and murder
above the quiet death
that has seized the world
Ur-forest natives elephants
swarms in the sea
and in the air and even
the air itself
Significant play
of rising and falling words
Cadences
which make no poor man rich
no rich man wiser
no wise man
capable of acting justly

Hovering images like smoke
a play as of fire
while underneath
wood senselessly destroys itself.

Dem Gedicht auflauern

Hinter dem Mond
mag es daheim sein oder
vertrieben aus etwelchem Bewußtsein
Es schleicht sich ein
in Versammlungen
seine Farben wechselnd
ein Chamäleon

In Träumen ist es wach
aber ungreifbar
rätselhaft wie die Welt
und ebenso sinnlos
zugehörig einer Gattung
die ausstirbt
leichtfüßig dahingeht
kaum erfaßt um sogleich
in deinem Gedächtnis
eindeutig leblos
zu werden

Pursuing the Poem

At home perhaps
behind the moon or
driven from whatever consciousness
It sneaks
into assemblies
changing its color
like a chameleon

Awake in dreams
but intangible
puzzling like the world
and as meaningless
belonging to a race
now dying out
moving off lightfootedly
scarcely grasped when
it becomes
unequivocally lifeless
in your memory

Vom Dorotheenstäkdtischen Friedhof

Auf den Friedhöfen der toten Dichter
triumphiert die Macht
über die Ohnmacht des Wortes

Selbst schwere Steine
sind nur leichtfertige Lügen
erhaben über wehrlosem Gebein
Barrikaden gegen die Lebenden
damit sie hier einhalten
im Denken und wissen
daß sie anheimfallen
der weiterwährenden Gebrauchsfähigkeit
früher oder später

Besucher wie du
im dunklen Anzug und mit erforderter Miene
vernehmen niemals die Warnung
das erbärmliche Geschrei welker Blätter
unter den Sohlen auf dem Wege
zum zugewiesenen Platz.

At the Dorothea State Cemetery

At the cemeteries of dead poets
power triumphs
over the impotence of words

Even heavy stones are
no more than frivolous lies
rising above defenseless limbs
barricades against the living
that they may stop here
in thought and know
sooner or later
a continuation of their usefulness
will run out

Visitors like you
in dark suits and with the required mien
rarely perceive the warning
in the piteous screams of faded leaves
beneath the soles on the way
to the appointed place.

Zu Dürers "Hieronymus im Gehäuse"

Im Vordergrund ruht
abwesend ein müder Löwe blicklos
daneben dicht
ein Hund im Schlaf
Perspektivisch ferner sitzt
in der dargestellten Stille seiner Kammer
der Heilige
vor seinem Pult und schreibt
irgendetwas auf Papier: Womöglich

Das Unerahnte

Das Wort
das die Zielbetrogenen vergaßen
das alles in sich birgt
was Geborgenwerden meinte
Gerettetsein im grauen Licht
das durch die Butzenscheiben
endlos strömt.

On Durer's Hieronymous

In the foreground
a tired lion rests absent unseeing
a sleeping dog
close at his side
In the perspective's distance
the Saint sits
in the painted quiet of his room
and at his desk writes
something on the paper: Perhaps

The unimaginable

The word
forgotten by disillusioned idealists
that in itself holds everything
meant by sheltering
salvation in the gray light
that endlessly streams
through the window pane.

Eine Poetik

Das wahre Gedicht
löscht sich selber aus
am Schluß
wie eine Kerze so plötzlich
aber was sie beleuchtet hat brennt
das abrupte Dunkel
der Netzhaut ein

Kahle Welten
Kahle Wände Tische und Stühle
ein Raum voller fremder Bekannter
unserer Zuneigung und Gleichgültigkeit
gewiß

Ohne Bewegung ohne Bedeutung
ohne Bestand.

A Poetics

The true poem
extinguishes itself
at the end
like a candle so suddenly
but what it had lit burns
within the abrupt darkness
of the retina

Bare worlds
Bare walls tables and chairs
a room full of strange familiars
knowing
our inclinations and indifference

without movement without significance
without weight.

EPILOGUE

Letter to a Reader

Since you asked to know something of the way I work I must confess that the most laborious part takes place in the morning, namely the rising: an Olympic accomplishment in the masterful skill of weight lifting, for example, the raising of eyelids: both eyes torn open at the same time only to be closed immediately on facing the bright light. Everything else the day may contain in the way of problems and activities can be faced with confidence and on lighter shoulders which are fixed and supported, held firmly by small claws: writing, as long as it remains free of woodenness and routine, will not relax its hold on the writer. Nevertheless, a remnant of uncertainty exists as to what it is one is driving at—and what is driving one. Is it really a matter of sublimation of raised genitals, or an excessive compensation for failure to gain the boxing championship? Is writing the one and only ordering principle to which an otherwise chaotic psyche clings for some bit of certainty? Is there some basis to the belief that writing is really an equivalent for other things which have passed one by—or are steadily passing by? Blind spots, white spaces on the total map of the author's being, his way of existing here and now, the contents and meaning of which he cannot himself know. I suspect an author has his difficulties with the author for whom there is a strong case of a shared identity. For the belief can easily be shaken: in the psychological search for the basis of his literary existence the author cannot be entirely certain (not after Kaspar Hauser[1] and Gantenbein[2]) that he must necessarily be *he*. Every pre-school child at one time or another questions his own existence, not understanding why he is a child of such or such an age when he could just as well be a flower or a St. Bernard: to no avail to be sure. In contrast to the author for whom such a question leads, as we know, to the work of art. What dangers an author faces—his personality which he assumed to be an historical given, again and again turned upside down, and his professional ethos with its single-minded goal troubled by all sorts of uncomfortable doubts: a kind of widening chink in consciousness. He wants to change the world, yes, but he has already failed in every other profession; he serves humanity, but certainly not without recompense, and while he identifies with humanity, a large part of the population resents him; he, a strong egocentric who has no clear image of himself is critical in his work of egocentric positions; he presumes to spread the light of a new truth never suspecting that truth cannot be distributed; either it already exists as a root in the universal consciousness and literature can only activate it, or it is not present in consciousness and then no matter how strong the claim to truth it will not be understood. Or only after thirty years have passed. But to despoil paper for the sake of being honored thirty years later as the single visionary is hardly enough to make for a sound moral, or even

---

[1]Because of his mysterious origins and checkered career Kaspar Hauser was given various problematical identities in several literary works of the 19th century.

[2]MEIN NAME SEI GANTENBEIN (My name is Gantenbein) is the contemporary work of Max Frisch who grants this name to a diffuse "I," moving in various directions to wards various destinies.

pragmatic basis for literature. It may be that threadbare excuses provide the only reasons for this special activity, and for this letter there may be only one, namely that you, dear reader, asked for it.

OHIO UNIVERSITY LIBRARY

Please return this book as soon as you have finished with it. In order to avoid a fine it must be returned by the latest date stamped below.

MAR 1989

CF